Night
of Botswana

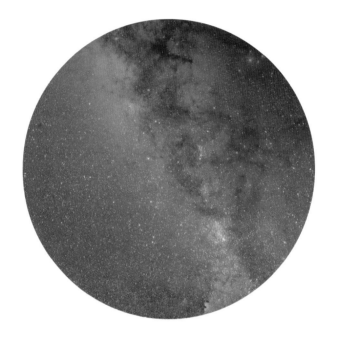

Stephen O'Meara

For Deborah
My Heaven on Earth

Published by Struik Nature
(an imprint of Penguin Random House South
Africa (Pty) Ltd)
Reg. No. 1953/000441/07
The Estuaries No. 4, Oxbow Crescent, Century
Avenue, Century City, 7441
PO Box 1144, Cape Town, 8000 South Africa

Visit www.penguinrandomhouse.co.za and join
the Struik Nature Club for updates, news, events
and special offers.

First published in 2020

10 9 8 7 6 5 4 3 2 1

ISBN 978 1 77584 693 2 (Print)
ISBN 978 1 77584 736 6 (Epub)

Copyright © in text, 2020: Stephen James
O'Meara
Copyright © in photographs, 2020: Stephen James
O'Meara, unless otherwise specified alongside
individual images
Copyright © in illustrations, 2020: Stephen James
O'Meara
Copyright © in published edition, 2020: Penguin
Random House South Africa (Pty) Ltd

Publisher: Pippa Parker
Managing editor: Roelien Theron
Editor: Natalie Bell
Designer: Gillian Black
Proofreader: Thea Grobbelaar
Indexer: Steve Anderson

Reproduction by Studio Repro and Hirt & Carter
Cape (Pty) Ltd
Printed and bound in China by 1010 Printing
International Ltd.

MIX
Paper from
responsible sources
FSC
www.fsc.org
FSC® C016973

Front cover: Heart of the Milky Way
Title page: Heart of the Milky Way looking
towards Sagittarius
Contents page and back cover: The Pleiades
Star Cluster

Acknowledgements

No book is written without the support of others. This book started life as a research project
about the southern stars over Botswana, and the lore of the indigenous people. I had a
Botswana Government Research and Filming Permit, which, together with the support of
Botswana's Immigration Department, allowed me to stay in the country as a resident while
giving me access to many of the country's parks during this years-long project.

I am ever grateful to the following people: Deborah Carter of Yoga Safari; Vince Higgs of
Cambridge University Press; Mike Holding and Tania Jenkins (TJ) of Afriscreen, who guided me
through the process and introduced the original concept to the government; Peter Michaud
of Gemini Observatory, my editor and best friend in Hawaii (my former homeland); Deborah
Peake of Mochaba, who introduced me to some of the local storytellers; and Professor Susan
Ringrose – who I think of as family, the Former Director of the Okavango Research Institute. I
would also like to thank the team at Penguin Random House in South Africa, especially their
Nature publisher, Pippa Parker, who believed in the book and guided it on its way; Natalie
Bell for her effectual editing and suggestions; Gillian Black for her elegant design; and Colette
Stott for her stellar photo research. Finally, I am indebted to the living descendants of the early
Basarwa people, who offered their knowledge of the traditional sky.

Deborah Carter offered me much more than a letter of support – she offered me a home
and her heart. She was by my side throughout the process – which was not always a simple
undertaking. Without Deborah, this book would not exist. Now I am pleased to say that in
July 2017, she also joined me as my wife ... and best friend. Thank you, Deborah.

Contents

INTRODUCTION

The southern Milky Way with the dark Coalsack Nebula visible.

Night Skies of Botswana is a simple guide to visual astronomy for novice stargazers. Visual astronomy is the study of the night sky using the human eye, with or without optical aids like binoculars. Anyone, anywhere, can become a visual astronomer – all it takes is a sense of wonder and a desire to learn more about the skies above.

Botswana is well known as a premier tourist destination. The Okavango Delta – a fragile wetland system and UNESCO World Heritage Site – harbours some of the world's most endangered species of large mammals. What is less known is that much of the Botswana wilderness is the perfect natural environment for enjoying another wonder: the star-filled night sky, complete with the Southern Cross (one of the most sought-after constellations in the skies), the Eta Carinae Nebula (a monstrous cloud of gas and dust harbouring a supergiant star some four million times more luminous than the Sun), the Large and Small Magellanic Clouds (two dwarf galaxies being torn apart by our Milky Way) and so much more.

People who see these wonders under natural, dark sky conditions are fortunate, because the natural sky is globally threatened by light pollution, making the stars – or the way we see them from Earth – an endangered phenomenon. Bright artificial light at night infiltrates the sky, washing starlight away from view. It is estimated that 80% of the world's population lives under skyglow – the unnatural brightening of the night sky due to poorly shielded lighting. The brighter the sky appears at night, the fewer stars can be seen. Fortunately, much of Botswana is free from light pollution – especially in and around the Central Kalahari Desert, Okavango Delta and other pockets of low-density population – and the stars may be seen here in their diamond-like purity, much as they appeared to the indigenous people of Botswana in times gone by.

The indigenous people of Botswana saw the stars long before astronomers did; their interpretations of the skies appear throughout the book in the form of star lore.

Light pollution: a threat to wildlife

Not only does artificial light mask the bounty of stars from our sight, it can confuse plants and animals that rely on the natural cycle of night and day. Poor artificial lighting can have deadly effects on many creatures, especially prey that rely on the cover of darkness to avoid detection. Wetland habitats, which are home to frogs (whose night-time croaking is part of their breeding ritual), are adversely affected by light pollution. Lighting directed upward into the sky can cause birds that rely on the Moon and stars for navigation to wander off course. Gross overuse of lights has also caused a decline in insect populations, negatively impacting all predatory species that rely on insects for food or pollination.

Flying insects are attracted to artificial lights, removing them from other ecosystems. Lighting also causes insects to die from exhaustion or fall victim to predators. If you must use outdoor lighting, make sure it has a low wattage and proper shielding, so that it does not beam into the sky.

These images show the same region of sky taken from two different locations. **Top:** The sky free from light pollution as seen from Botswana's Samadupi Pan. **Bottom:** The ill effects of Maun skyglow as seen from a densely populated region just north of town. Skyglow from Maun – the main gateway to the Okavango Delta – is already visible from many safari camps within 100–160 kilometres of this tourism centre, threatening the natural appearance of this World Heritage Site. Excessive and misdirected night-time lighting reflects off airborne dust, smoke and other particulates in the air, scattering the light and washing away starlight. As the population of Botswana grows, light pollution will increase in the coming years, unless people take measures to adopt proper night-time lighting.

Stargazing in the southern hemisphere

You can use this book at any time of year, from anywhere south of the equator. The star charts featured were created for stargazing from Botswana (at latitude –20° south), and at the times given at the top of the charts. Readers farther north of this latitude will see the stars near the northern horizon a little higher than they appear on the charts, and the stars near the southern horizon a little lower to the horizon. The opposite will be true for readers farther south.

The stargazer's tools

The basic tool of the astronomer is the eyes, followed closely by star charts, which are essentially maps of the sky. The star charts give views of the night sky from each cardinal direction (north, south, east and west) for every month of the year, from 20:00–22:00. The focus is on the brightest stars, some well-known constellations, and the very brightest nebulae and clusters visible to unaided eyes.

Almost all star charts are computer generated. All the star charts here are based on original drawings and show a personal view of the night sky in its simplest form. They were redrawn on my computer and their apparent colour and brightness were incorporated. Everyone perceives star colour differently, so don't be alarmed if you see little or no colour when you look at the night skies, or a variation of the colour that appears in this book.

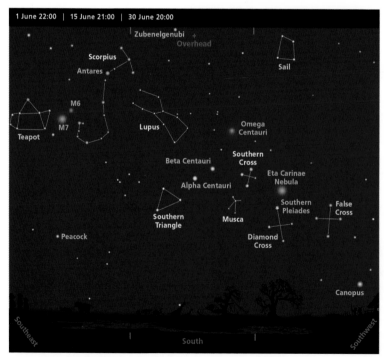

A star chart for June shows the southern sky at a glance.

Star lore in the star charts

The stories that the indigenous people of Botswana, the Basarwa, have told about the stars for generations appear throughout the book. In some cases, I have created constellation figures to help envision what they saw. I have also used my imagination, in the tradition of ancient stargazers the world over, to create figures of common animals and objects that may be more familiar to users in Botswana.

For instance, while people living in the northern hemisphere may be familiar with a Native American myth imagining the Big Dipper as a Great Bear being followed by three Native American Indians, the view from Botswana can just as easily be imagined as cattle being herded by three locals; we can even add in their dogs (two conspicuous stars nearby, traditionally known as the Herding Dogs).

I also incorporate more globally familiar figures based on Greek, Roman and other classical mythologies. In many instances, I've used some neo-classical representations of the constellations, adapted from *Urania's Mirror* (see box below). I encourage you to find your own patterns among the stars. All over the world, our predecessors rejoiced whenever stars rose in the east before sunrise, believing they contained the souls of their ancestors. In a way, many skywatchers today continue that tradition by looking at the stars as companions in the night. And it is that feeling of companionship that I wish to share with you in this book. Even if you learn the name of just one star, then writing this book will have served its purpose.

Urania's Mirror

Urania's Mirror is a boxed set of 32 star charts first published around 1825. They have been attributed to a Reverend Richard Rouse Bloxam (1765–1840) of the Royal Astronomical Society. He apparently created the cards to aid in the teaching and learning of the constellations. This collection has been called 'one of the most charming and attractive of the many aids to astronomical self-instruction'. The original set had a unique design: holes punched in the positions of bright stars allowed the user to hold any card up to a light and compare the star pattern with the constellation figure. It was an ingenious and hands-on approach to learning.

Cards for Aquarius (top) and Taurus (bottom).

Practical stargazing tips

◆ **Dress appropriately:** Spending an hour or more outside under a clear night sky can be chilly unless you are prepared. Dress warmly in layers, especially during winter. Take a blanket, just in case.

◆ **Apply insect repellent** to ward off bugs.

◆ **Pack creature comforts** such as food, beverages and accessories, and take a portable table.

◆ **Take good company:** Stargazing is an activity best done in the company of people you enjoy.

◆ **Select a proper location:** If you live in an urban environment, consider driving to a viewing location away from city lights. If you want to observe from home, turn off all indoor and outdoor lights. Select an observing spot where lights from the neighbourhood do not interfere with your vision.

◆ **Alleviate neck strain:** Looking up at the sky for prolonged periods of time can lead to neck strain. Consider using a reclining chair with a blanket and pillow. Recline the chair to an angle between 30° and 45° for maximum benefit.

◆ **Know your directions:** Ensure that you know the cardinal directions (north, south, east and west) from the observing site, to read the star charts properly. (Astronomers call compass directions 'azimuth'.) A star's height above the ground is called its altitude, measured from the ground (0°) to the point overhead (90°), which is known as the zenith. If an astronomer says that a certain star lies 45° high in the **eastern** sky after sunset, the stargazer will know that it is halfway between the ground and the zenith, looking **east**.

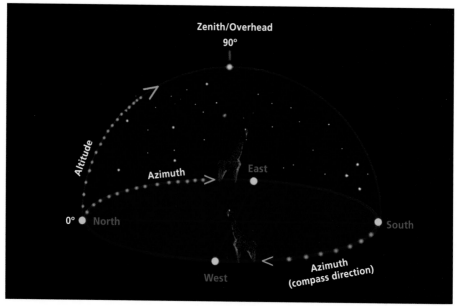

Stargazers must know the directions from their observing site, and they should also understand the appropriate orientation terminology.

◆ **Avert your gaze:** Night-sensitive rod cells and day-sensitive cone cells line the retina at the back of the human eye. The 120 million or so rod cells occupy the retina's periphery. We see faint celestial objects best when we look out of the corner of our eyes (averted vision). All skywatchers use this technique, sometimes referred to as peripheral vision.

◆ **Use binoculars:** This book is meant for visual observing with unaided eyes and binoculars. Use a pair of binoculars if you can. See box at right for further information about binocular sizes.

◆ **Use a red torch** to read star charts at night (explained in the box below).

Practise your peripheral vision

Go outside and stare directly at a bright star, then look off to the side but keep your attention focused on the star. If you do it properly, the star should swell slightly in brightness. Now try the technique on a faint star – the result should be more dramatic.

Did you know?

Binoculars: know your numbers
Binoculars come in a variety of sizes. For viewing stars, a 7×35 or 7×50 pair of binoculars is recommended; they are light enough to hold without causing arm strain. The number 7 refers to the number of times the image is magnified, while the number 35 or 50 refers to the diameter in millimetres of the lenses at the front of the binoculars.

Why do you need a red torch?

www.ultrafire.com

Red torches help our eyes to read star charts in the dark. There are two types of light detectors at the back of our eyes: rod cells and cone cells. Rod cells work best at night, in low light; cone cells function best during the day. When we move from a well-lit space into a very dark one, our cones essentially shut down, but our night-sensitive rods do not start seeing well immediately. (Anyone who has been outdoors on a bright sunny day then moved into a dark indoor room has experienced temporary night blindness.)

The rod cells' ability to see well at night depends on a photochemical called rhodopsin. When rhodopsin is exposed to bright light, it 'bleaches out', making the rods temporarily ineffective in a dark environment. It takes about 30 minutes for the photochemical to regenerate and make the rod cells effective. Astronomers say it takes about 30 minutes for our eyes to dark-adapt fully. Tests have shown that eyes that have dark-adapted for 30 minutes are six times more sensitive to light than eyes that have dark-adapted for only 15 minutes.

Avoid reading the star charts with a bright white light or torch; the intense glare will temporarily ruin your ability to see faint stars. Fortunately, our eyes are insensitive to red light, so, if you can, read the star charts using a torch with a red filter. Alternatively, use a dim light source, or cup your hands over the torch beam to allow just a little bit of light through.

About this book

This book is structured as follows:

◆ **Getting to know the night skies:** This section introduces important terms and concepts used by stargazers around the world.

◆ **Monthly star charts:** There are 48 star charts, showing views of stars in the north, south, east and west for each month of the year. You can start at any month; it doesn't matter.

◆ **Our solar system:** Dip in here for information about the Sun, the Moon, the planets and other bodies such as meteors, comets and 'space junk'.

◆ **Appendix:** All stars and deep-sky objects described are listed, along with the month in which they are explained; see page 180.

Label colours

Labels on all the star charts have been colour-coded as follows:

White: general labels and constellation names
Blue: planets and asterisms
Green: deep-sky objects including star clusters, nebulae, galaxies and variable stars
Yellow: star names

Measuring the sky

You can measure angular distances in the night sky with your hands. Stretch out your arm to full length and close one eye.

Measuring 10°
Hold up a fist with your thumb resting on top of your index (pointing) finger. The amount of sky your fist covers measures approximately 10°. This is roughly equal to the length of the False Cross.

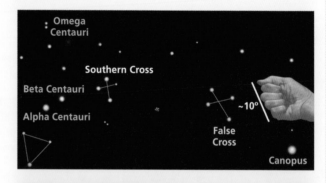

Measuring 20°
A relaxed hand with an outstretched little finger and thumb covers approximately 20°. This is roughly equal to the distance between the right side of the Southern Cross and the left side of the False Cross.

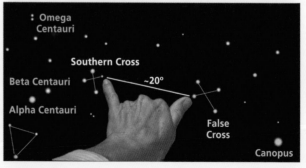

How to use the star charts

1. Page to the month when you plan to observe the night sky.
2. Select a viewing direction (north, south, west and east). Dividing the sky in this way will help those who only have a clear view in one direction, such as from a bush camp. The example below shows the most prominent stars in the northern skies visible on 1 January at 22:00, 15 January at 21:00 and 31 January at 20:00.
3. Within each month, the **northern** and **southern** views of the night sky are discussed in more detail than the western and eastern views.
4. Star names and constellations are printed in **bold**, and a guide to pronouncing the name follows in *italics* afterwards.

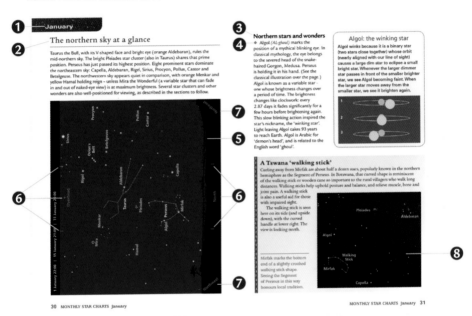

30 MONTHLY STAR CHARTS January

MONTHLY STAR CHARTS January 31

5. A silhouette of a Botswana landscape at night helps to scale the view in each star chart. Star colours shown are based on personal observations. They have been exaggerated to stand out in print. Keep in mind that everyone sees colour slightly differently.
6. Red text at the top and bottom of the star charts helps with orientation.
7. Red words printed diagonally in each bottom corner of the star charts are there to assist with orientation. Simply turn the chart until the diagonal word is horizontal. That will give you the proper sky orientation for that direction. When you turn the chart, the illustrated horizon will also tilt, but ignore that – just focus your attention on the orientation of the stars.
8. Additional star charts and photographs show smaller regions of the sky in more detail.

GETTING TO KNOW THE NIGHT SKIES

The southern sky, looking towards the Large Magellanic Cloud, with bright Canopus to its upper right and the Milky Way arching overhead.

On dark, moonless nights, the stars dominate the skies above. They shine and shimmer like distant campfires and, to the observer, can feel just as warm and inviting. But all these burning specks are very distant – so far away that they hide their true nature. Each speck of starlight is a gigantic ball of burning gas called a sun – like our Sun, which is also a star. Our Sun shines so brightly because it is the closest star to the Earth. The next closest star visible to the unaided eyes at night is Alpha Centauri, one of the two bright Pointer Stars that direct us to the Southern Cross.

Light years apart!

It is of no use to describe the distance to the stars in kilometres or miles – they are just too far away. Instead, astronomers use a measure called the light year. Light travels at a phenomenal speed – some 300,000 kilometres in one second. In a single second, light can travel around the Earth seven times!

Light from Alpha Centauri takes a long time to reach our eyes – about four years. Thus we describe Alpha Centauri as being about four light years away.

The Milky Way

All the stars you see in the night sky are part of the Milky Way – the galaxy in which we live. It is an immense island of stars, dust and gas, measuring about 100,000 light years across. We can also see other galaxies in the night sky with our unaided eyes. They do not appear as stars, however, but rather as diffuse glows.

The Milky Way is a magnificent, multi-armed spiral galaxy, containing some 200 to 400 billion stars, of which our Sun is just one. Our solar system, which contains our Earth, is nested between two spiral arms – well away from the galaxy's centre. Remarkably, our galaxy is only one of billions and billions of other galaxies in the universe.

Astronomers refer to the flat disc of the Milky Way as the plane of the galaxy; it is the 'highway' around which our Sun, with all the other stars in the Milky Way, travels as it orbits the galaxy's centre. Moving at the fantastic speed of approximately 220 kilometres per second, it will take our Sun about 250 million years to complete one orbit around the galaxy.

The band of milky light that stretches across the night sky is not the entire Milky Way Galaxy, but just a part of the thin disc as viewed edge-on from Earth.

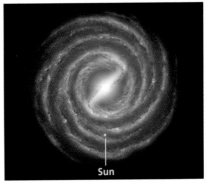

Sun

NASA

NASA's interpretation of what the Milky Way Galaxy probably looks like when viewed from above – a magnificent spiral made up of billions of stars.

Right: The dense band of stars that we see as the Milky Way is just one arm of the immense spiral of the Milky Way Galaxy.
Below: An artist's impression of the side view of the Milky Way. Note the flat disc and central bulge.

Bulge

Disc

Infrared Processing and Analysis Center/ Caltech & University of Massachusetts

Patterns and constellations

Astronomers have divided the night sky into 88 areas with official boundaries. These areas contain the star patterns we know as constellations. The identified constellations have been handed down to us through the ages by people of different cultures – most notably the ancient Babylonians who lived in what is now Iraq, as well as by the Greeks and Romans. The constellations in the southern hemisphere were named much later (from the fifteenth to around the middle of the eighteenth century), many by European navigators and explorers.

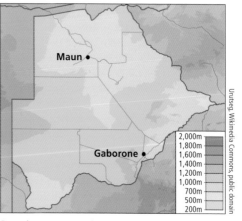

Star charts are similar to geographical maps. In this example, Gaborone and Maun lie within the boundaries of the region we call Botswana.

Celestial boundaries are much like the official borders of different countries, within which we find our modern cities and towns. Similarly, the stars Betelgeuse and Rigel, for example, lie within the boundaries of the region of sky we call Orion.

This book does not refer to celestial boundaries, as they are not visible boundaries. Instead, the star charts identify only the brightest stars in a constellation. The outline of familiar 'star patterns' is also sometimes shown and labelled.

In this star map, the white area defines the boundaries of the constellation Orion, with stars within.

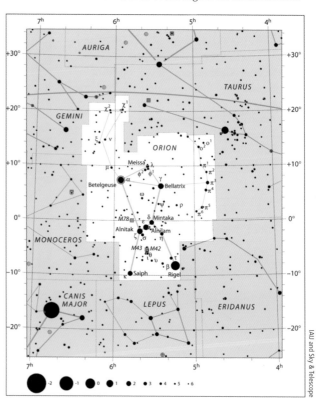

The stars

Star colour

Stars not only look like distant campfires, they have something else in common: colour. Just as the hottest part of a flame appears blue-white, so too do the hottest stars appear blue-white to our eyes; and just as the coolest part of a flame appears orange-red, so too do the coolest stars appear orange-red.

Stars are grouped according to colour (or spectral type). The coolest stars burn at temperatures of around 3,000 °C.

The table below gives examples of some well-known bright stars, displaying their spectral range and average temperatures.

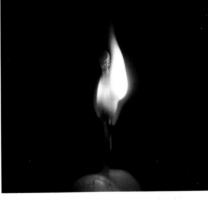

You can tell how hot a star is by looking at its colour – just as you can with a burning flame. This image shows a lit match, with the hottest part (blue colour) appearing at the base of the flame, and the coolest part (red colour) appearing at the tip.

Star	Colour	Average temperature
Rigel	Blue-white	12,000°C
Canopus	Yellow-white	6,750°C
Alpha Centauri	Yellow-orange	5,500°C
Aldebaran	Orange-red	3,700°C
Antares	Red	3,250°C

Stars have different colours. Alpha Centauri (the bright star at the far left) is pale yellow. The top star in the Southern Cross (the four bright stars on the right) is more orange, while other bright stars in the frame are blue-white.

Star magnitude

A star's brightness depends on the amount of light it emits and its distance from Earth. Astronomers refer to a star's brightness as its magnitude, and it is measured in numbers as follows: a star of 0 magnitude (very bright, visible to the naked eye) is 100 times brighter than a star of 5 magnitude (roughly the faintest star our eyes will see). As most stars have positive magnitudes, astronomers generally do not use a plus sign (+) to show positive magnitudes. A luminous star very far away may appear only as bright (or even fainter) as a less luminous star that is closer to Earth. Two basic rules help to understand magnitude:

Rule 1: The greater the positive number, the fainter the star.
Rule 2: The greater the negative number, the brighter the star.

The four brightest stars in the sky have negative magnitudes: Sirius (−1.45); Canopus (−0.62); Arcturus (−0.05); and Alpha Centauri (−0.01).

> **Did you know?**
>
> The Full Moon is magnitude −13; the Sun is magnitude −26.

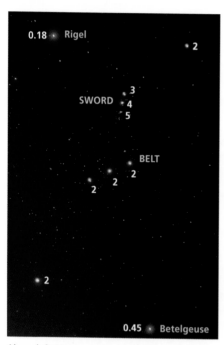

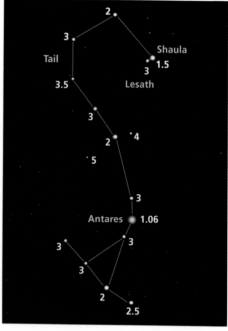

Above left: Star magnitudes in the constellation of Orion. The stars in Orion's Belt are similar in appearance but the middle (supergiant) star is farther away than the outer two. **Above right:** Star magnitudes in Scorpius. Shaula (one of the Stinger stars at the tip of the Scorpion's tail) is a hot-blue star, six times larger than our Sun and 365 light years distant; its fainter Stinger companion (Lesath) is more than twice as large but it is also much farther away (520 light years).

Star names

Most of the brightest stars have been given names (e.g. Betelgeuse) and have a Greek letter associated with them. Generally, the brightest star in any given constellation is known as Alpha (first letter in the Greek alphabet); the second brightest star is known as Beta (second letter in the Greek alphabet), and so on. Alpha and Beta Centauri (the Pointer Stars to the Southern Cross) are the brightest and second-brightest stars in the Centaurus constellation. An Omega object, on the other hand, like Omega Centauri, is at the faint end of vision. This is only a general rule, there are exceptions.

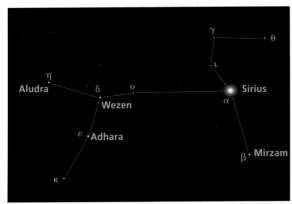

The order of stars in Canis Major (the Greater Dog) does not follow the general rule. Its second brightest star (Adhara) bears the designation Epsilon (the fifth Greek letter), while its third brightest star (Wezen) bears the Greek letter Delta (fourth in the alphabet). This ancient interpretation of the sky divided the right and left parts of the constellation into two different star patterns.

The 25 brightest stars in the night sky

1. Sirius (–1.45)
2. Canopus (–0.62)
3. Arcturus (–0.05)
4. Alpha Centauri – Rigil Kent (–0.01)
5. Vega (0.03)
6. Capella (0.08)
7. Rigel (0.18)
8. Procyon (0.40)
9. Betelgeuse (0.45)
10. Achernar (0.45)
11. Hadar – Beta Centauri (0.61)
12. Altair (0.76)
13. Acrux – bottom star of Southern Cross (0.77)
14. Aldebaran (0.87)
15. Spica (0.98)
16. Antares (1.06)
17. Pollux (1.16)
18. Fomalhaut (1.17)
19. Deneb (1.25)
20. Mimosa – left star of Southern Cross (1.25)
21. Regulus (1.36)
22. Adhara – in Canis Major, the Greater Dog (1.50)
23. Castor (1.58)
24. Gacrux – top star of Southern Cross (1.59)
25. Shaula – bright Stinger Star in Tail of Scorpion (1.62)

Did you know?

The Greek alphabet

The characters of the Greek alphabet are used by astronomers to label the stars.

α	alpha	η	eta	ν	nu	τ	tau
β	beta	θ	theta	ξ	xi	υ	upsilon
γ	gamma	ι	iota	ο	omicron	φ	phi
δ	delta	κ	kappa	π	pi	χ	chi
ε	epsilon	λ	lambda	ρ	rho	ψ	psi
ζ	zeta	μ	mu	σ	sigma	ω	omega

The planets

If you look up at the night sky and see a bright star that you cannot identify on the monthly star charts, then it is probably a planet. Planets do not twinkle as much as the stars – they shine with a steadier light.

The planets move, little by little, through the stars each night, which is why ancient stargazers called them 'The Wanderers'.

The five naked-eye planets may appear as some of the brightest stars in the night sky. They orbit our Sun and shine by reflecting sunlight. Their apparent brightness can vary greatly as they travel around the Sun – moving close to or away from the Earth. For example, Mars can, at times, be as bright as magnitude –3 when it is closest to both the Earth and Sun, but as faint as 2 when furthest away. The average brightness values of the naked-eye planets are as follows:

The motion of Mars illustrated for two dates in 2018. Note how Mars appears brighter on 17 July, when it was closer to the Earth and Sun.

◆ Mercury 1.5
◆ Venus –4
◆ Mars –0
◆ Jupiter –0
◆ Saturn 0

The zodiac

Viewed from Earth, the Sun, Moon and planets circle the sky along a narrow band of sky called the zodiac. The word 'zodiac' means 'circle of animals'. Ancient astronomers divided the zodiac into twelve zodiacal constellations: Aries (the Ram), Taurus (the Bull), Gemini (the Twins), Cancer (the Crab), Leo (the Lion), Virgo (the Virgin), Libra (the Scales), Scorpius (the Scorpion), Sagittarius (the Archer), Capricornus (the Sea Goat), Aquarius (the Water Bearer) and Pisces (the Fishes). Libra is the only exception in the zodiac because it is not an animal but rather inanimate scales. However, it was once considered to be the claws of the Scorpion.

The zodiac is a narrow band of sky divided into twelve zodiacal constellations.

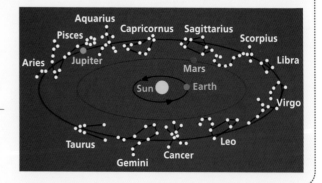

This image was taken on the night of 5 August 2016, when all five naked-eye planets (also called 'The Wanderers') and the Moon were visible, tracing a line along a section of the zodiac.

The deep sky

In addition to the stars and the planets, the stargazer may see a variety of clusters, nebulae, galaxies and more – collectively known as deep-sky objects. There are five main categories of deep-sky objects described in this book:

◆ **Variable stars** are stars that change brightness over time. Some are visible to the naked eye for short periods of time before they dip below naked-eye visibility. Some pulsate over days or months whereas others may suddenly flare into view.

◆ **Open star clusters** are physically related collections of stars (held together by gravity). These stars travel together in the same direction through space. An example is the Pleiades.

◆ **Globular star clusters** are densely packed spheres of starlight – some comprising up to a million stars. They are the largest, oldest and most massive objects in our galaxy.

The Pleiades are an open star cluster.

Globular star cluster.

Catalogues of deep-sky objects

Deep-sky objects are known by a variety of names, some based on the initials of the catalogues in which they appear. Here are some of the most prominent catalogues and examples of stars they contain:

Messier Catalogue (M) The Orion Nebula is also known as M42. The M stands for the last name of Charles Messier (1730–1817), an astronomer who included the Orion Nebula as the 42nd object in his now-famous catalogue.

New General Catalogue (NGC) The Pin Cushion star cluster is also known as NGC 3532 – meaning it is the 3,532nd object in the *New General Catalogue*.

Index Catalogue (IC) The Southern Pleiades star cluster is also known as IC 2602, the 2,602nd object listed in the IC.

DEEP-SKY COMPANIONS

The Messier Objects

Second Edition

Stephen James O'Meara

Cover image of a book in the Deep-Sky Companions series.

Above left: Orion Nebula; Above right: The Coalsack Nebula looks like a dark cloud.

◆ **Nebulae** are giant clouds of dust and gas in space. They come in two varieties: bright and dark. Bright nebulae appear to the eye as diffuse patches of ghostly light, such as the Orion Nebula. Dark nebulae are clouds of dust that appear in silhouette against bright nebulae or along the Milky Way. The aptly named Coalsack Nebula near the Southern Cross is an example of a dark nebula.

◆ **Galaxies** are sometimes called island universes. The Milky Way is the galaxy in which our Earth is situated. Galaxies are unfathomably large collections of stars, gas and dust – all swirling around a centre of gravity. They can contain billions of stars. Only a few galaxies – such as the Large Magellanic Cloud – can be seen without optical aid.

The Large Magellanic Cloud is one of the few galaxies that can be seen with the naked eye.

As the Earth turns

The Earth spins on its axis once every 24 hours. From Earth, however, it is the sky that appears to turn like a giant wheel, at a speed of 15° every hour. As a result of the turning Earth, the stars appear to march across the sky as night progresses. In general, a star rising in the east shortly after sunset will be setting in the west shortly before sunrise.

Left: The camera shutter was open for an extended period of time, which created a photograph showing star trails caused by the Earth's rotation. Because of the 'movement' of the stars across the sky, the monthly star charts are valid only for specific dates and times, as given on the top strip of each chart.

Below: Orion's movement from east to west over the course of a night is evidence of a slowly turning Earth.

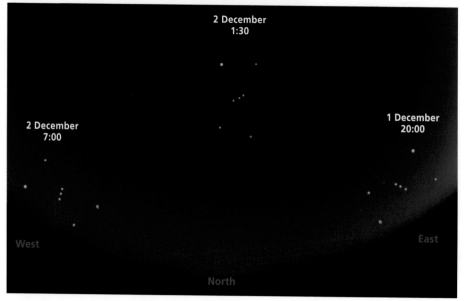

2 December
1:30

2 December
7:00

1 December
20:00

West

East

North

Seasons of stars

The Earth spins on its axis and travels around the Sun simultaneously. It takes the Earth 365 days (one year) to complete one orbit, or one journey around the Sun. Each day, as the Earth travels in its orbit, we see the stars and constellations rise four minutes earlier each night. Consequently, we see the stars from a slightly different perspective each night.

This time adds up over the course of weeks and months. As the illustration below shows, if Orion is rising in the east after sunset on 1 December, it will be high in the north after sunset on 1 March. Three months after that, on 1 June, Orion will be setting in the west shortly after the Sun. This shifting of position is used in an ancient Greek legend concerning Orion – a mortal hunter and giant among men – and Scorpius, the Scorpion.

The story of Orion

One day, Orion chanced upon Artemis, daughter of Zeus and goddess of the hunt and the Moon, bathing in a pool. They instantly became friends and fell in love. Artemis's twin brother Apollo couldn't believe his sister would fall in love with a mere mortal. Jealousy surged through Apollo's veins, and drove him to send a giant scorpion to kill Orion while he slept. But Orion awoke in time to battle the fantastic creature, escaping by swimming out to sea. Not to be outdone, Apollo ran to his sister and told her a lie; he said a traitor to their lands was trying to escape by swimming away. Artemis reacted quickly. She grabbed her bow, ran to the water's edge and took aim. She fired an arrow that pierced the heart of the swimmer. Only then did she realize she'd been fooled and had killed her beloved. To honour Orion, the Moon goddess raised Orion into the night sky and placed the Scorpion opposite him, so that its sting could never reach her friend. That's why, whenever we see Orion rising in the east, the Scorpion is setting in the west, and vice versa.

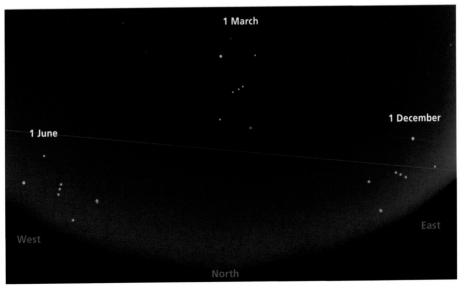

Orion is shown shortly after sunset, on three dates, moving across the sky as the year passes.

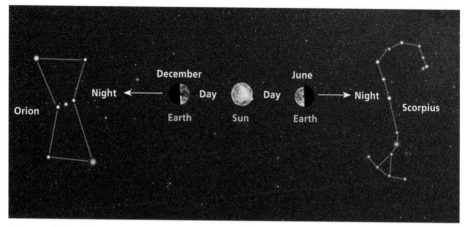

Orion and Scorpius are always directly opposite one another in the sky. In June, when the Scorpion is in the night sky, Orion lies directly opposite (in the direction of the Sun), making it invisible from Earth. The reverse is true in December, when Earth has moved halfway around the Sun in its orbit. In December, Earth's night side faces Orion, and its day side faces Scorpius (making the Scorpion invisible).

Did you know?

Dung beetles navigate with the stars

At night, a dung beetle uses light from the Moon to help it on its way. Entomologists from South Africa and Sweden discovered that when the Moon is absent from the sky, dung beetles use the light of the Milky Way to orient themselves along straight paths as they roll their balls of dung.

Dung beetles have very sensitive compound eyes that can detect individual stars as well as the hazy path of the Milky Way. To orient themselves, they climb on top of their dung ball and perform an 'orientation dance'.

While humans, birds and bats use bright stars as navigational guideposts, the dung beetle provides the first documented use of the Milky Way Galaxy for orientation in the animal kingdom.

On moonless nights, dung beetles use light from the Milky Way to navigate as they roll their balls of dung.

Botswana's Basarwa star lore

Throughout the ages, human beings have developed their own cosmology, or stories, to explain the origin of the universe. Across the world, many tales have been told about the twinkling lights and dark depths of the night skies.

Botswana's Basarwa have their own star stories, some of which are featured in this book.

The Basarwa are a group of people whose origins date back some 70,000 years. Their cosmology was handed down orally. Very little has been written down, but anthropologists have found some stories describing the significance of the stars that are common to all Basarwa. One such tale explains how the night sky was made of blue stone, punctured with holes. After sunset, the Sun would travel from west to east over the top of this stone ceiling. Sunlight shining through the holes created the stars.

Basarwa mainly used the stars to record the passage of the night and seasons. Sometimes stars were used for navigation.

Today, people living close to the land in Botswana sometimes use bright stars to help them find their way at night. They might use a bright star on either side of them to guide them home. Then, as the months pass and the 'guide stars' move to new locations in the sky, they choose new beacons to show the way.

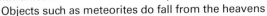

Did you know?

Stones fall from the skies

Bored stones (with a hole in the middle) are a familiar artefact to most southern Africans. Archaeologists tell us that these stones were used as weights on sticks, to assist with digging. But the Basarwa of southern Africa have a different understanding. They believe that 'sky beings' dropped small, doughnut-shaped rocks to Earth. These stones had special powers: to shamans, the hole was a portal to another realm. In Botswana, these stones are called *Lentswe la Badimo* – 'stones of the ancestors'. They were used to beat the ground near the graves of the ancestors, to communicate with those who had passed.

In Botswana, bored stones are seen as a gift from the ancestors.

Objects such as meteorites do fall from the heavens – and some have impacted Botswana. Could it be that some indigenous people long ago witnessed the fall of a meteorite, only to find these strange-looking bored stones in a place where they thought a stone from the sky might have fallen?

Venus glows at night: early indigenous people of Botswana knew Venus by two names.

Venus

Early indigenous people in Botswana divided the night sky into night and dawn stars. For this reason, they saw Venus as two stars. As the 'evening star' they called it *Kopadilalelo* ('seeker of supper'); as the 'morning star' they called it *Naledi ya Masa* ('time to rise') or *Mphatlalatsane* ('brilliant one'). If *Kopadilalelo* was not visible when they ploughed their fields, they anticipated drought. If it was visible, they believed their harvest would be good. To the Bakalanga people of northeastern Botswana, Venus was *Megalilangote*, which is the name of the stick used to stir porridge, perhaps due to the planet's slow 'stirring' motion as it rises and falls towards the Sun over time.

Some early inhabitants of Botswana perceived the stars as spirits of the ancestors.

Spirits in the sky

Some indigenous people of Botswana saw the stars as spirits of the dead. A star's brightness signified the importance of a particular person when he or she was alive. The longer a person was dead, the fainter a star would appear. This belief meant that newly deceased people and animals could shine more brightly in the sky. Others believed that the stars were the spirits of those unwilling to be born.

The serpent in Tsodilo Hills

Take a walk around the Tsodilo Hills, a World Heritage Site in the northwest corner of Botswana. There is a megalithic 'snake' poking what looks like its head out of a cave. A series of ritual indentations collectively resembling snake skin is carved into the rock's natural serpent shape. This rock has been interpreted as a representation of the sacred python from which humankind descended. The serpent is arguably the most widespread mythological creature known to humanity and, in many cultures around the globe, represents the Milky Way. It may well be that this snake-shaped rock is one of the earliest records of the Milky Way.

A megalithic 'snake' inside a cave in Tsodilo Hills is thought to represent the Milky Way.

The Milky Way

The milky band of hazy light we call the Milky Way was known by the Basarwa as *Molalatladi* ('path of rain and thunder' or 'place where lightning rests') or *Molalakoko* ('neck of a chicken'). Today, some know it simply as *Selemela* – a group of stars. In early times, the Milky Way was seen as a source of guiding light.

The Milky Way was also imagined to be the 'backbone of the night', the 'sky's spine' or 'God's back'. These interpretations suggest that the Basarwa saw the Milky Way as central to the structure of their visible universe. It was also envisioned as a supernatural footpath that their spirit ancestors used to cross the sky. It's possible that these early inhabitants of Botswana were some of the first people to think abstractly, meaning they had the ability to ponder objects, principles and ideas not physically present.

In one Basarwa legend, a girl who wished to help hunters journey home by night threw wood ashes into the sky to guide them on their way; these ashes then became the Milky Way.

The Milky Way, looking towards the centre of the galaxy between Scorpius and Sagittarius. Dark dust lanes slice through the flat disc while the galaxy's large oval bulge of stars is seen at upper left.

MONTHLY STAR CHARTS

The northern sky at a glance

Taurus the Bull, with its V-shaped face and bright eye (orange Aldebaran), rules the mid-northern sky. The bright Pleiades star cluster (also in Taurus) shares that prime position. Perseus has just passed its highest position. Eight prominent stars dominate the northeastern sky: Capella, Aldebaran, Rigel, Sirius, Procyon, Pollux, Castor and Betelgeuse. The northwestern sky appears quiet in comparison, with orange Menkar and yellow Hamal holding reign – unless Mira the Wonderful (a variable star that can fade in and out of naked-eye view) is at maximum brightness. Several star clusters and other wonders are also well positioned for viewing, as described in the sections to follow.

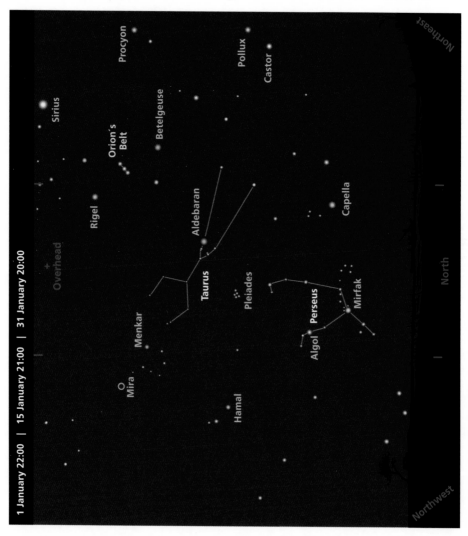

Northern stars and wonders

◆ **Algol** *(AL-ghoul)* marks the position of a mythical blinking eye. In classical mythology, the eye belongs to the severed head of the snake-haired Gorgon, Medusa. Perseus is holding it in his hand. (See the classical illustration over the page.) Algol is known as a variable star – one whose brightness changes over a period of time. The brightness changes like clockwork: every 2.87 days it fades significantly for a few hours before brightening again. This slow blinking action inspired the star's nickname, the 'winking star'. Light leaving Algol takes 93 years to reach Earth. Algol is Arabic for 'demon's head', and is related to the English word 'ghoul'.

Algol: the winking star

Algol winks because it is a binary star (two stars close together) whose orbit (nearly aligned with our line of sight) causes a large dim star to eclipse a small bright star. Whenever the larger dimmer star passes in front of the smaller brighter star, we see Algol becoming faint. When the larger star moves away from the smaller star, we see it brighten again.

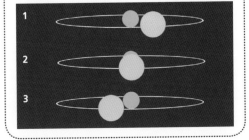

A Tswana 'walking stick'

Curling away from Mirfak are about half a dozen stars, popularly known in the northern hemisphere as the Segment of Perseus. In Botswana, that curved shape is reminiscent of the walking stick or wooden cane important to those rural villagers who walk long distances. Walking sticks help uphold posture and balance, and relieve muscle, bone and joint pain. A walking stick is also a useful aid for those with impaired sight.

The walking stick is seen here on its side (and upside down), with the curved handle at lower right. The view is looking north.

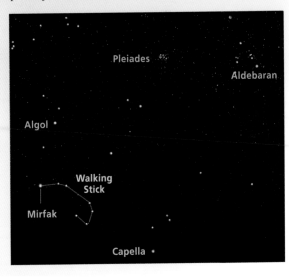

Mirfak marks the bottom end of a slightly crooked walking stick shape. Seeing the Segment of Perseus in this way honours local tradition.

◆ **Mirfak** *(MEER-fak)* is the alpha (brightest) star in the constellation Perseus the Hero. In ancient Greek mythology, Perseus rescued the Chained Maiden, Andromeda, from the gaping jaws of Cetus the Sea Monster (also known as the Whale). It lies in a lovely stream of stars that arcs towards the Pleiades. Mirfak is part of another open star cluster known as the Alpha Persei Cluster. So star clusters and bright stars rule January's northern sky.

◆ **The Alpha Persei Cluster** is very low in the Botswana sky. Its brightest member, Mirfak, is a yellow-white

Mirfak in the constellation Perseus the Hero.

supergiant star about 120 times larger than our Sun. Several of the cluster's stars can be spied without optical aid. The view in binoculars (shown at right), however, can be stunning on clear nights. Light leaving the cluster takes about 570 years to reach our eyes. In other words, it is 570 light years away.

◆ **Taurus the Bull** is best identified by its face: a prominent V-shaped pattern between Orion and the Pleiades, punctuated by the bright orange star Aldebaran. You can cover this V with three fingers held at arm's length. The full bull constellation, however, is much more sprawling than that, with extremely long horns and a partial body comprised of dim stars. The illustration below helps to picture the upside-down bull, with the body defined by rather dim stars.

Mirfak – the brightest star in the Alpha Persei Cluster: look for a serpentine chain of bright and faint stars.

Right: The body of Taurus, supporting the long horns, is made up of dim stars. **Below:** Bright-orange Aldebaran helps stargazers to find Taurus the Bull.

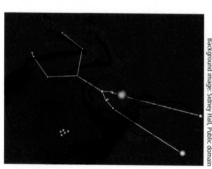

Aldebaran and Hyades

Aldebaran is the brightest member in a V-shaped grouping of stars called the Hyades. All the stars in the Hyades, except for Aldebaran, are part of an open star cluster that moves through space like a flock of birds. Aldebaran appears to be part of the flock, but that is an illusion – it is two times closer to Earth than the cluster. Aldebaran just happens to lie along the same line of sight – just as the fish eagle in the photograph (far right) is much closer to the camera than the flock of birds.

Aldebaran looks bigger than the Hyades, just as the fish eagle in the foreground (above right) appears bigger than the birds in the background. Aldebaran is in fact two times closer to Earth than the cluster.

◆ **Pleiades** *(PLEE-eh-deez)* or **M45**. To the lower left of Aldebaran is the ghostly glow of the Pleiades open star cluster. These stars form a family: they were born together, travel together, and are bound by gravity. Romantics over the ages have imagined their glittering form as a rosette of diamonds, shining dewdrops, and a swarm of fireflies, to name but a few descriptions. To others, the grouping looks like a little dipper. Classically known as the Seven Sisters of Atlas – upon whose shoulders the vault of the heavens rests – the Pleiades is one of the brightest and closest star clusters in the entire sky. A marvel to behold with unaided eyes, their stellar beauty is unrivalled when seen through binoculars. The stars were born only 100 million years ago – when dinosaurs ruled the Earth.

Plough with the Pleiades

The Basarwa knew the Pleiades as *Selemela*, which means 'cultivator'. The Pleiades was an important group, because whenever it was seen shining overhead in the early evening, it was a signal to start planting. Botswanans today begin cultivating crops in early November.

The Pleiades may be seen as a mob of meerkats.

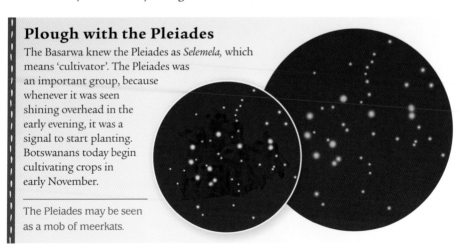

The southern sky at a glance

The southern sky looks tranquil when compared with its northern counterpart. Three prominent and colourful stars surround the mid-southern sky: yellow Canopus, blue Achernar and Acamar (the latter two in Eridanus the River). Beneath this triangle lie the delicate Large and Small Magellanic Clouds (LMC and SMC, respectively). The small Cloud lies on the western flank of a fainter equilateral triangle of stars that defines the boundaries of Hydrus the Male Water Snake. To its upper left is the little southern diamond known as Reticulum. Sirius burns brightly in the eastern sky. Three crosses occupy the low southeastern sky: the Southern Cross and its celestial masquerader (the False Cross) are the two best

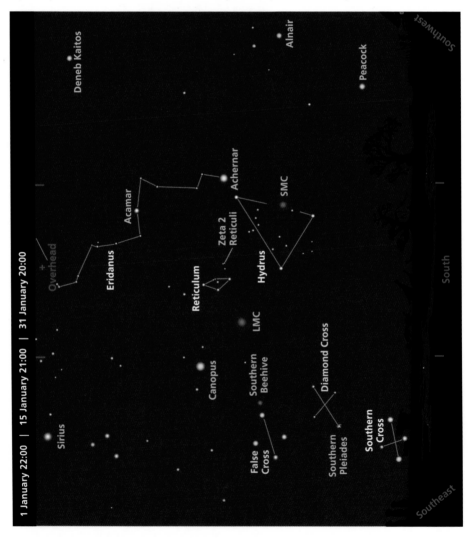

known; the third is the little-known Diamond Cross, which lies roughly midway between them and a tad south. Low in the southwest, we find two pale blue stellar gems – Peacock and Alnair – sailing slowly towards the horizon with warm-hued Deneb Kaitos farther north.

Did you know?

Zeta Reticuli is home to the 'Greys'

In September 1961, Betty and Barney Hill were driving through the White Mountains of New Hampshire in the United States when they saw a bright light close to the Moon, following their car. Barney looked at the object through binoculars and saw a large craft with alien beings grinning at him through a window. The Hills sped home, but lost two hours of time that they could not explain. Fearing something might have happened to them, they sought professional help a year later, and that is when their abduction story began.

Under hypnosis, both Hills told tales of being abducted by small greyish-coloured beings (the 'Greys') who performed medical examinations on them. The alien leader showed Betty a star map that included our Sun and the star of the aliens' home planet. Five years later, school teacher Marjorie Fish analysed Hill's map, and after six years and 23 unprofitable attempts to match Hill's map to a three-dimensional model of the stars closest to the Sun, she finally found a plausible solution and identified Zeta Reticuli as the home star of the 'Greys'.

While some ufologists believe Fish's work proves the reality of the Hills' abduction account, professional astronomers trying to replicate Fish's three-dimensional star model (using data far superior than the half-century-old information Fish used) were unable to validate her theory. A University of Illinois astronomer and professor emeritus, Jim Kaler, sums up the situation by saying, 'Seems unlikely'.

Whether you believe these claims or not, it's intriguing to look upon the stars and imagine the possibility of other life forms 'out there'. Are we alone? We still do not know the answer, but the rapid rate of discovery of extrasolar planets is increasing the chance of encountering other life forms.

The author interviewed Betty Hill in the USA in 1981. She sketched the star map for him, shown to her by the Greys' 'leader'. This reconstruction of her map shows the key stars she drew under hypnosis, complete with trade routes (solid and dashed lines, also reconstructed) allegedly used to and from Zeta Reticuli. Labels of this star system and our Sun have been added to aid identification.

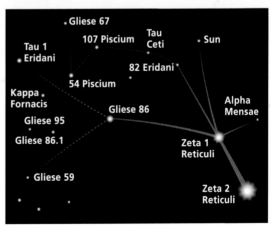

Southern stars and wonders

◆ The three brightest stars of **Hydrus the Male Water Snake** form a striking equilateral triangle. It is a relatively modern constellation, named in the late sixteenth century by Dutch navigators. Hydrus is called the Male Water Snake to differentiate it from the more northerly and larger constellation Hydra the Female Water Snake, described in March. The shape of the snake can be seen using the stars within and near the triangle.

◆ **Reticulum** is a small and relatively modern constellation described in the 1750s. It represents a diamond-shaped, silk-threaded reticle – an optical instrument that early telescopic observers used to measure star positions. From a scientific perspective, Zeta 2 Reticuli is a sun-like star with a sizeable cloud of icy dust surrounding it. Is there an Earth-like planet orbiting that star? If there is, it will be situated in an orbit similar to that of our Earth around the Sun. Earth-based technologies and space telescope missions in the future may soon provide an answer.

◆ **The Large and Small Magellanic Clouds** (LMC and SMC, respectively) are named in honour of the Portuguese navigator, Ferdinand Magellan, who described them in 1519 – although many ancestral people across the southern hemisphere recorded them much earlier. They are not clouds at all, but satellites (mini-galaxies) that orbit our Milky Way. The Milky Way's tidal forces are slowly tearing the Magellanic Clouds apart. Binoculars will show the LMC's and SMC's warped structures, as well as some of their individual stars, nebulae and open star clusters. Most prominent in the LMC is the Tarantula Nebula. It is easy to spot with the naked eye or without optical aids.

Left: The Large and Small Magellanic Clouds are mini-galaxies that orbit our Milky Way.
Below: The Tarantula Nebula in the Large Magellanic Cloud is easy to spot with the naked eye.

Basarwa lore of the Magellanic Clouds

The Magellanic Clouds played a significant role in Basarwa lore. The Large Magellanic Cloud (LMC) was *Kgoro* and the Small Magellanic Cloud (SMC) was *Tlala*. If *Tlala* (the fainter of the two) was consistently clearly seen, then it was said that a drought was near; if *Kgoro* was clear, then plentiful rains were expected. During drought, the air is dusty, which dims celestial objects. Rains clear the air of dust, making celestial objects appear clearer.

To some Basarwa of the Kalahari, the Magellanic Clouds were patches of thornless grass, which made a soft bed. They were a favourite hunting spot for God, as they gave God an expansive view. Others saw the Clouds as male and female steenbok (LMC and SMC, respectively). Still others said the Large Cloud was 'The Spoor of the Horn Star' (Canopus) and the Small Cloud was the 'Spoor of the Little Horn Star' (Achernar).

Above right: The Small Magellanic Cloud is seen with the globular star cluster, 47 Tucanae. This view can be seen with a good pair of binoculars.
Right: Some regard the Magellanic Clouds as a male and female steenbok.

The eastern sky at a glance

Sirius, the brightest star in the night sky, sparkles in the mid-skies like a scintillating diamond. Lemon-coloured Canopus, its second in command, lies to the right (southeast) at a distance of about three fist-widths (turn the chart to show this correct orientation). Note how the Belt of Orion points towards both Sirius and orange Aldebaran. The straw-coloured Alphard and Procyon bracket the Head of Hydra the Female Water Snake, now low in the eastern sky. You will need an unobstructed horizon to see it. Pollux and Castor, the Twin stars of Gemini, lie low in the northeast.

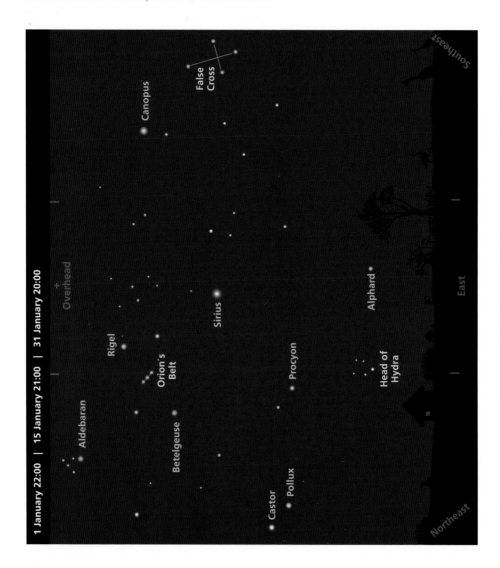

The western sky at a glance

Deneb Kaitos, the tail of Cetus the Sea Monster, holds the prime viewing spot in the mid-western sky. It is outshone by bluish Achernar far to the left, and equalled in brightness by modest Hamal, equidistant to the right – unless the variable star Mira is visible (see December for a detailed description). The Great Square of Pegasus star pattern will be the first to slip below the western horizon as the night progresses, followed by the Circlet of Pisces, and the bright star Fomalhaut.

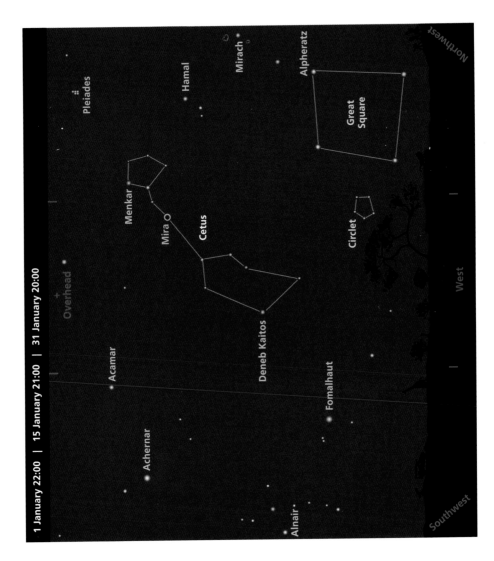

The northern sky at a glance

The seven bright and colourful stars forming a large hexagon in the sky now dominate the northern celestial landscape. (Note how the hexagon forms a ring around rose-coloured Betelgeuse.) Chief among the hexagon's stars is Sirius, the brightest star in the night sky – it lies at the pinnacle of the heavens. A line drawn through Orion's Belt, pointing to the upper right, will guide you to Sirius and in the opposite direction to orange Aldebaran. Regulus in the Sickle of Leo the Lion is rising in the eastern sky, along with golden Alphard in Hydra the Female Water Snake (described in more detail in March), while Mirfak and Algol in Perseus are slipping towards the northwestern horizon.

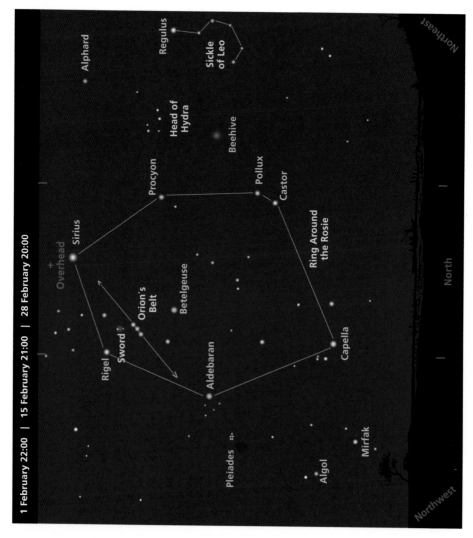

Northern stars and wonders

◆ **Sirius** *(SEER-ee-us)*, or **Alpha Canis Majoris**, is the brightest star in the night sky. Its name comes from the Greek word meaning 'sparkling' or 'scorching', and refers to its scintillating beauty. Sirius is unrivalled in brilliance because it lies so close to our Sun; it is only about nine light years away. In classical depictions, Sirius, also known as the Dog Star, marks the snout of Canis Major, the Greater Dog of Orion the Hunter. The Egyptians worshipped Sirius as the Nile Star; whenever Sirius rose in the east before the Sun, the Nile River overflowed, fertilizing the thirsty soil. According to Seiss's *Gospel in the Stars*, Sirius represents the coming of the Messiah.

Sirius marks the hottest time of the year in the northern hemisphere, giving rise to the phrase 'dog days of summer', referring to the 20 days before and after Sirius aligns with the Sun and they rise and set together. Ancient Romans believed the star generated the heat during this time. The phrase has taken on new meaning in recent times – in fact it has nothing to do with hot dogs or mad dogs; it simply refers to the presence of the Dog Star.

Did you know?

The Gospel in the Stars

Written by Joseph Seiss, an American theologian and Lutheran minister, it was first published in 1882. The work looks upon the twelve signs of the zodiac as signs of Christian symbolism. Seiss opens his work saying, 'The sublimest visible objects of human contemplation are the Starry Heavens'. According to Seiss, Sirius represents the coming Messiah.

Sirius the leader

The Basarwa saw Sirius as a chief star called *Kgogamasigo*, meaning 'one that pulls the night across'. It was depicted as a leader of the heavens. Sirius is so bright that people believed it pulled the other stars across the sky with it as the night progressed, but this is just an illusion caused by the Earth's rotation.

In South Africa's Cape region, the indigenous people believe that when Sirius is 'in the Sun's warmth' (most likely referring to when the star makes its first appearance before the Sun), it is time for the women to go out in the early morning to gather termite eggs for food.

Who let the dogs out?

Tswana people knew Orion as *Dintsa le Dikolobe*, meaning 'three dogs' (Sword) 'chasing three warthogs' (Belt). Warthogs have their litters while Orion is prominent in the sky – frequently litters of three.

◆ **Belt of Orion (Orion's Belt)** To the upper right of Aldebaran lies Orion, with three close and moderately bright stars – lined up like three ducks in a row – forming its Belt. In the Bible, Job refers to the Belt stars as the 'bands of Orion'; they are also known as the 'three kings', referring to the Magi who sought out the Christ child in the Christian Christmas story.

While Orion's Belt is one of the most recognizable star patterns in the skies, it is more than a random gathering of stars. Like the Hyades and Pleiades, the three Belt stars belong to an open star cluster that lies in a region of space where new stars are still being born.

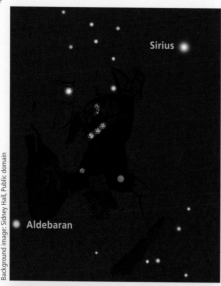

Background image: Sidney Hall, Public domain

Sirius

Aldebaran

Orion the Hunter

In classical mythology, Orion was a mighty hunter and a giant among men. He is seen in the sky holding a club and lion-skin shield, facing Taurus the Bull, with whom he battles. Skywatchers in the southern hemisphere see many of the classical constellations upside down, especially when looking north. The line of three faint stars that represents Orion's Sword appears to extend upward like an arrow shot into the Hunter's heart, rather than a sword dangling from his belt.

Left: Orion the Hunter is seen upside down from southern Africa.
Below left and right: View of Orion from the northern and southern hemispheres.

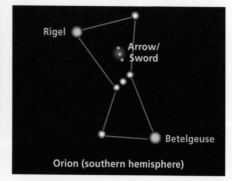

Orion (northern hemisphere)

Orion (southern hemisphere)

Southern Orion

The rainmaker

The Basarwa may long ago have known Betelgeuse as *Serogabolo*, which means 'rain'. When Betelgeuse was overhead in the evening, it was believed that rain would fall. In Botswana this belief still holds true today, but rain has become associated with Orion because of Betelgeuse's proximity to this constellation. When Orion is rising in the east after sunset, the rainy season usually begins; it lasts until March, when Orion is overhead.

The animals

Some Kalahari Basarwa today imagine the corner stars of Orion as male steenbok and the three Belt stars as female steenbok. Orion's Sword is imagined to be duiker.

Orion's Belt Cluster

To the ancient Maya, the Belt of Orion was the centre of creation. In a way, they were right: Orion's Belt was once an active centre of star birth. Seen through binoculars, the three bright belt stars – and the twisting, serpentine strings of fainter stars around them – were all created from the same cloud of dust and gas in space. Light from this cluster takes about 1,200 years to reach our eyes. All of its stars move together through space, like a pack of wild dogs (the stars moving somewhat more peacefully than their canine counterparts).

The magic of Orion's Sword

Under dark skies, avert your gaze and look for a misty light surrounding the middle star in Orion's Sword. If you see it, you will be looking 1,500 years back into time, at a glowing cloud of dust and gas birthing stars. This stellar nursery is called the Orion Nebula and is one of the few that can be seen without optical aid, although the binocular view (right) is much more spectacular.

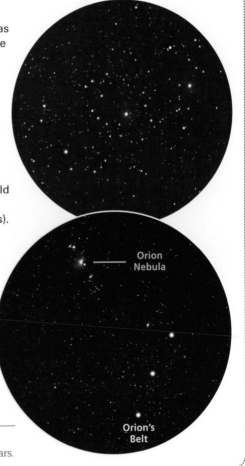

Top: Orion's Belt viewed through binoculars.
Right: Orion Nebula viewed through binoculars.

An early tale of Orion from southern Botswana

One day, the wives (the Pleiades) of the sky god (Aldebaran) asked their husband to go out and hunt – and not return unless he was successful. Taking his bow and only one arrow, the great god climbed atop the Large Magellanic Cloud, which was full of soft grass on which he could lie and wait. From that lofty perch, he sighted three zebra (the Belt of Orion). Raising his bow, he took aim, but suddenly noticed a lion (Betelgeuse) waiting in the grass. His fingers slipped and the arrow (Sword) fired, missing the zebra. Too afraid to retrieve his arrow in the presence of a hungry lion, and too ashamed to return to his wives without food, the hunter remains where he is, eternally afflicted with thirst, hunger and shame.

◆ **Rigel** *(RYE-jell)* is the brightest star of Orion and the seventh brightest star in the night sky. It marks one of Orion's feet and shines with a pale blue light. Although it looks like a big pinprick to the naked eye, Rigel is actually a supergiant star. If we could reel it in like a fish and place it next to our Sun, it would appear nearly 150 times larger in comparison and shine 85,000 times more brightly!

◆ **Betelgeuse** *(BEEtle-juice)* marks the armpit of Orion. Like Rigel, Betelgeuse is a supergiant star, but much older and cooler, so it shines with a reddish-orange light. Unlike Rigel, Betelgeuse is a variable star and pulsates (swells and contracts) over the years without any known regularity. We see the pulses as slight changes in the star's brightness. Sometimes it rivals Rigel in brightness; other times it's a bit fainter, similar to Aldebaran (which ranks fourteenth in brightness).

◆ **Capella** *(KA-pell-a)* Drop your gaze below Aldebaran and you will see charming Capella, the sixth brightest star, twinkling yellow-gold in the low northern sky. Capella is an ancient Arabic name meaning 'little she-goat', and the

In an early Botswanan tale, the wives (Pleiades) of the sky god (Aldebaran) await his return, unaware that he has lost his arrow.

star was seen as the beating heart of that imaginary animal. In India, Capella was worshipped as the heart of the creator god, Brahma. The triangle of three smaller stars immediately to the upper left of Capella represents three of the little she-goat's kids. This month Capella is moving away from its highest point in the sky, as seen from Botswana and southern Africa.

◆ **Auriga** *(or-EYE-gah)* Capella is the brightest star in the constellation of Auriga, the shepherd who in classical mythology cared for a little she-goat and her kids. The brightest stars in the constellation form a hexagon, so we have a small hexagon of stars within the larger hexagon displayed on our chart. Most early cultures across the globe imagined Auriga's stars as a wreath, while others imagined a death laurel on a grave. It would not be amiss to imagine Auriga as a kraal (enclosure for cattle), which is of significance to the local herders.

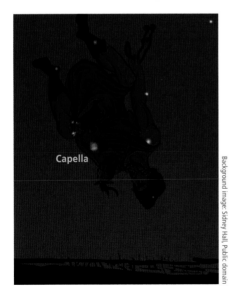

Auriga is seen as an upside-down shepherd when viewed from Botswana.

Capella, bringer of water

The green leaf horn

Some early people of the Western Kalahari called Capella the 'green leaf horn', because flowers bloomed when the star became visible with the coming rains. As seen in the northern star chart, Capella joins Orion during Botswana's rainy season.

The rain animal

The *Nyae Nyae !Kung* of the Kalahari saw Capella, together with the Pleiades and Canopus, as a mythical horned animal waiting for rain. The shape of the Pleiades undoubtedly resembled the face, while bright and colourful Canopus and Capella formed the horns. To other *!Kung*, Canopus was the male horn and Capella the female horn. This interpretation evokes an image of a great celestial beast – a 'rain animal' – facing eastward.

In this celestial scene, the bright reddish stars Betelgeuse and Aldebaran are lions, the hexagon of Auriga is a protective kraal, and stars within the fence are cattle (represented by only one cow here).

The southern sky at a glance

The two brightest stars in the night sky, Sirius and Canopus, preside over the south. They are noticeably different in colour: Sirius shines blue-white and Canopus displays a warmer yellow colour. Little Reticulum the Reticle, Hydrus the Male Water Snake and the Small Magellanic Cloud (SMC) have slipped farther away from the southern meridian (the imaginary line defining north–south). The Large Magellanic Cloud (LMC) is at its highest point in the south. The three crosses (Southern, False and Diamond) are gaining prominence in the southeast. You'll need a clear horizon to see Alpha and Beta Centauri low in the south-southeast, while Achernar and Acamar are sinking towards the southwest.

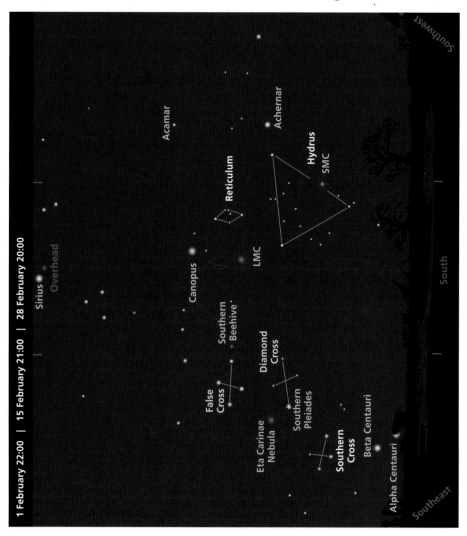

Southern stars and wonders

◆ **Canopus** *(can-OH-puss)* Canopus is the second brightest star in the night sky next to Sirius. It marks the position of the constellation Carina the Keel, which itself is part of an old constellation (no longer recognized) known as the ship Argo Navis. This giant yellow-coloured star is about 145 times larger than the Sun and about eight times as massive. When it finally exhausts its nuclear fuel, the star will pulsate until it violently collapses and explodes as a supernova – the final death throes of a massive star.

In ancient Greek mythology, Canopus is the name of a great navigator who guided a fleet of 1,000 ships to safety during a storm at sea. On that journey, King Menelaus had just rescued his wife, Helen of Troy, from a cowardly prince, when the storm blew his fleet off course. Canopus navigated the fleet safely to Egypt, where he died of a snake bite. Helen killed the snake, buried Canopus, and (as she was the daughter of Zeus) honoured Canopus with a place in the sky.

◆ **The Southern Cross** is a popular and much-sought-after star pattern within Crux the Cross – the constellation with the smallest area within its official boundaries in the night sky. No other part in the visible heavens draws as much attention as this region. Although the four stars of the Cross appear to be related, they are not – they all lie at different distances from the Earth: light from the Alpha star at the foot of the Cross takes about 325 years to reach our eyes, while light from the orange star at the head of the cross takes only 88 years.

Canopus the 'horn star'

The North Sotho of Botswana knew Canopus as *Naka*, related to *lenaka*, meaning 'horn of the beast'. Traditionally, the first sighting of Canopus was announced by blowing a gemsbok horn. In the past, it was tradition to begin the year when Canopus was first seen rising before the Sun in the southeastern sky. The first person to see the star would reputedly reap much maize. The arrival of the new year also heralded the windy season, and was a time when rainmaking ceremonies and initiation rites took place. The first initiate to sight Canopus would have good luck that year.

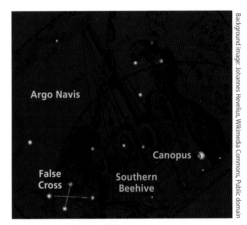

Canopus marks the keel of the ship Argo Navis.

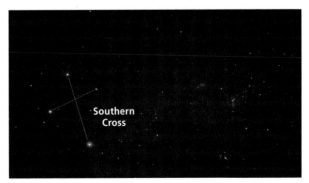

The Southern Cross lies in a rich swathe of the Milky Way.

A closer look at the Large Magellanic Cloud

The Large Magellanic Cloud (LMC) is a dwarf galaxy orbiting our Milky Way. Fantastic tidal forces are ripping it apart. You can see its tattered nature well in binoculars. Notice the beautiful cloverleaf-like Tarantula Nebula at left in the upper image. It is about 180,000 light years away.

Tidal forces acting on the Large Magellanic Cloud create its irregular shape.

NASA/Hubble Space Telescope

In this NASA/Hubble Space Telescope image, ribbons of gas (coloured pink in the image, but invisible to unaided eyes) have been stripped by the Milky Way from the Large and Small Magellanic Clouds (tiny white patches inside the pink ribbons) as they orbit.

The eastern sky at a glance

Sirius and Canopus preside over the high eastern sky, as they are near the zenith. The long form of Hydra the Female Water Snake is prominently placed in the east, along with its alpha star, Alphard. The Sail pattern of Corvus the Crow is now rising just south of east, though you will need a clear horizon to see it. The Sickle of Leo the Lion dominates the low northeastern sky.

Three prominent stars flank Sirius to the northeast: Procyon in Canis Minor (the Lesser Dog) and the Twin stars, Castor and Pollux, in Gemini.

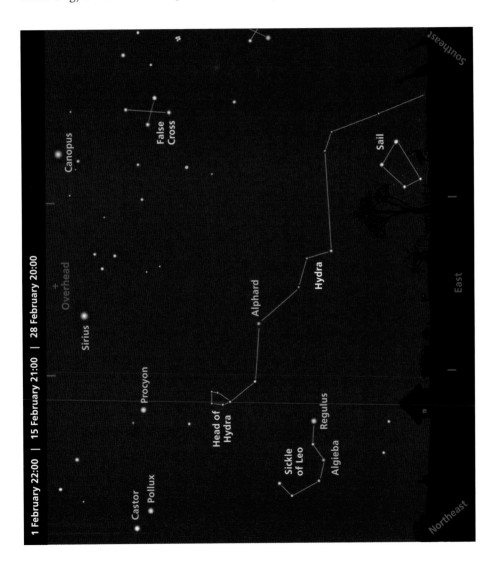

The western sky at a glance

Aside from our old friends Sirius and Canopus in the high western sky, we see a number of moderately bright stars closing in on the horizon. First to set will be Deneb Kaitos, extremely low in the west-southwest. This is the tail star of Cetus the Sea Monster, and it's looking redder now than usual because it is so low in the sky, where airborne dust can redden the view. Hamal in Aries will set later in the west-northwest. To its upper left, in the elliptical Head of Cetus, we find Menkar.

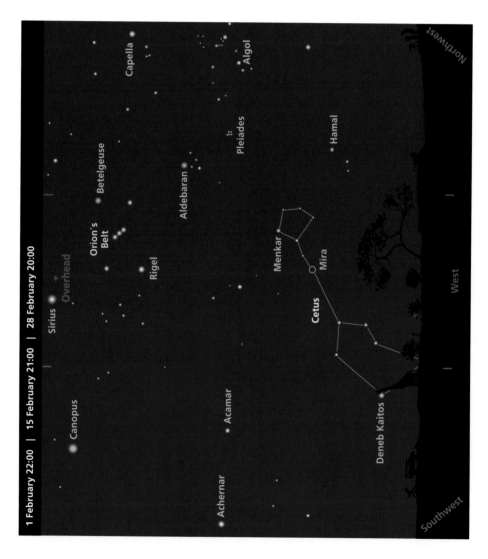

The northern sky at a glance

The Twin stars, Castor and Pollux, lie near their highest position in the north, while the Head of Hydra the Female Water Snake and its brightest star, Alphard, are in near pursuit. Sirius holds a supreme position nearly overhead. Yellow Capella, on the other hand, is getting ready to set in the northwest. Procyon and the Beehive open star cluster are now at their best for naked-eye and binocular viewing. The Sickle of Leo the Lion dominates the northeastern sky, with the bowl of the Big Dipper just starting to peek above that horizon.

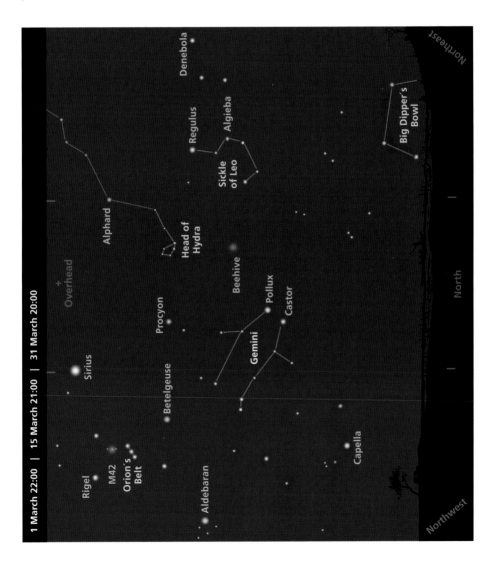

Did you know?

Castor and Pollux

Although Pollux slightly outshines Castor today, astronomers believe that either Castor was brighter once (but lost its lustre) or Pollux was fainter – no one knows. This may explain why early skywatchers stamped Castor as the constellation's alpha star. Today we know Castor is a white-hot star whose light takes 51 years to reach our eyes, while Pollux is a red giant 17 light years closer. And though you cannot see it, Castor does not shine with the light of a single star but of four stars packed closely together; Castor is a quadruple star system.

Northern stars and wonders

◆ **Alphard** *(AL-fard)* is the brightest star in the constellation of Hydra the Female Water Snake. It shines with a reddish glow and represents the snake's beating heart. Its name is Arabic for 'the solitary one', which reflects the star's lonely appearance in a quiet region of sky about two fists above Regulus. It is an orange giant star, some 120 times larger than our Sun. Light leaving its surface takes ~180 years to reach our eyes.

◆ **Castor** *(CASS-ter)* and **Pollux** *(POL-lucks)* In classical mythology, Castor and Pollux mark the heads of Gemini the Twins. They symbolize the equal day and night that occur each March when, from Botswana, they are high in the sky after

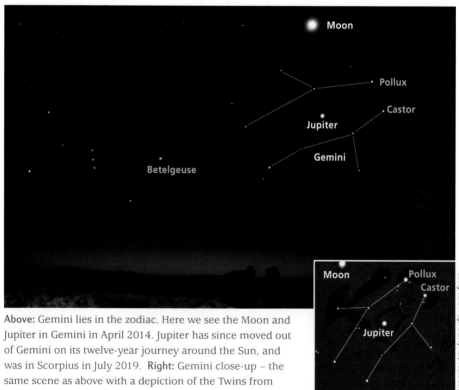

Above: Gemini lies in the zodiac. Here we see the Moon and Jupiter in Gemini in April 2014. Jupiter has since moved out of Gemini on its twelve-year journey around the Sun, and was in Scorpius in July 2019. **Right:** Gemini close-up – the same scene as above with a depiction of the Twins from *Urania's Mirror*.

Background image: Sidney Hall. Public domain

sunset around 21 March. In ancient times, Castor and Pollux were not human figures but kids (baby goats). They marked the third animal that the Sun visited in its yearly journey among the stars – the first two being Aries the Ram and Taurus the Bull.

◆ **The Praesepe** *(PRAY-suh-pee)*/**Beehive Cluster (M44)** If you are in the bush or under dark skies away from city and town lights at night, look about halfway up the sky above the northern horizon for the Beehive open star cluster. You'll also find it below the Head of Hydra (the Mud Hut) – about midway between Castor and Regulus. To unaided eyes, the cluster appears simply as a dim fuzzy glow. This foggy patch is also called the Praesepe, which refers to the straw in the manger of the Christ child – the manger itself being formed by four faint stars surrounding the Praesepe. The light we see left the cluster about 575 years ago.

Through binoculars this dim patch resolves into a busy swarm of starlight called the Beehive Cluster.

Castor and Pollux as guide stars

The Basarwa in the Kalahari have reported that, in March and April, their ancestors used Castor and Pollux in the western sky, together with Alpha and Beta Centauri in the eastern sky, to help guide them towards their village. By keeping Castor and Pollux to their right, and Alpha and Beta Centauri to their left, these two bright pairs of stars would steer them home after sunset.

During the author's stay with this community, the planet Jupiter was also rising brilliantly in the east after sunset in Virgo. The Basarwa explained that the 'star' was formed in the night sky by the embers of a distant fire, and that it would fade when the fire died down in the dawn, only to be reborn again the next night.

Left: Two bright pairs of stars, Alpha and Beta Centauri on the left and Castor and Pollux on the right, were used for navigation by the ancestors of the Basarwa.
Right: Jupiter's light is so bright that animals can use it to navigate.

◆ **Procyon** *(PRO-see-on)* is the brightest star in the constellation Canis Minor (Lesser Dog), one of Orion's two hunting dogs. The star lies about two fists either to the lower right of Sirius or to the right (east) of Betelgeuse. These three stars make a colourful equilateral triangle. Look for Procyon's gentle yellow hue. The star's name means 'before the dog', because, from the northern hemisphere, Procyon rises about 20 minutes before Sirius in Canis Major (Greater Dog). From Botswana, however, we see Procyon and Sirius rise together almost at the same time, with Sirius just ahead.

◆ **Hydra and the Mud Hut**
Classically, Hydra is the Female Water Snake with many heads; some star charts today depict Hydra with just one head. Hydra is also one of the twelve labours of Hercules.

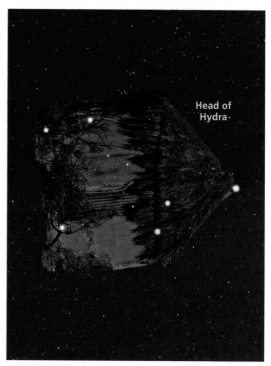

In March, the Head of Hydra looks like a mud hut lying on its side.

The red bird and the mud hut

In ancient China, the stars of the Head of Hydra formed the beak of the 'Red bird', a legendary bird similar to the Phoenix or Firebird. It had radiant feathers, an enchanting song and only appeared in times of good fortune.

Seen from Botswana, the Head of Hydra resembles a mud hut with a lopsided roof – we see the hut on its side at this time of night.

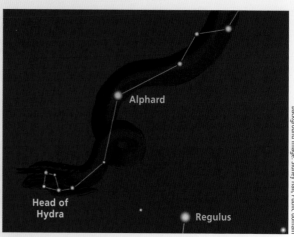

Hydra is depicted with just one head here, but in classical lore Hydra has many heads.

The southern sky at a glance

Canopus is still the most prominent beacon in the mid-southern skies. It is followed to the left by the False Cross star pattern and the Southern Beehive. The Large Magellanic Cloud (LMC) remains near its highest point in the sky, though its companion, the Small Magellanic Cloud (SMC), is near setting in the southwestern sky along with brilliant Achernar. Alpha and Beta Centauri (the Pointer Stars to the Southern Cross) are well placed now for viewing in the southeast. Between the False and Southern Cross lies the pale glow of the great Eta Carinae Nebula, the Diamond Cross, and the Southern Pleiades star cluster.

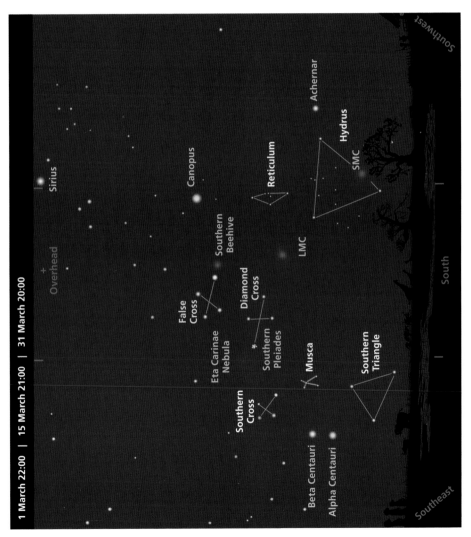

Four ways to find south

Polaris (also known as the North Star) in the northern hemisphere points the way to the north celestial pole. In the south, there is no single bright star to help us find the south celestial pole. However, there are other ways. Here are four different methods to find south:

Method 1

1 Draw an imaginary line from the star Gacrux at the top of the Southern Cross to Acrux at the bottom of the Cross.
2 Continue that line (from Acrux) and extend it 4.5 times farther; this will take you to a point 4° west of the south celestial pole.
3 Drop your gaze directly down to the horizon, and you'll be *close* to true south – close enough for you to get your general bearings.

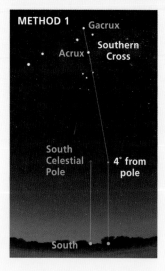

METHOD 1

Gacrux

Acrux

Southern Cross

South Celestial Pole

4° from pole

South

Did you know?

True south versus magnetic south

True south and magnetic south are not the same. True south is the direction one would travel on the Earth to reach the position of the Earth's south pole – the imaginary axis around which the Earth rotates. This position (in Antarctica at –90° latitude) lies directly beneath the south celestial pole – the point where the Earth's south polar axis, if extended indefinitely into space, would intersect the sky. A compass does not point to true south.

Magnetic south is the direction to which the south-seeking arrow of a compass points. It is the southern axis of Earth's magnetic field; it changes position over time.

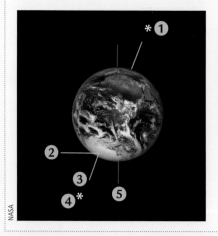

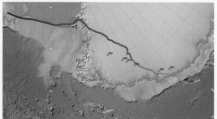

NASA

NOAA

Above: The south magnetic pole from 1590 (blue line at far left) to the present (yellow line at far right).

Left: **1** North celestial pole star; **2** True south; **3** South polar axis; **4** South celestial pole star; **5** Magnetic south pole (in 2020)

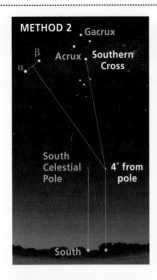

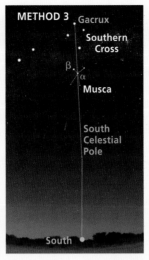

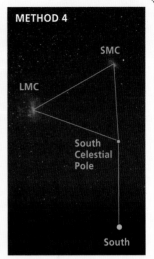

Method 2

Many skywatchers prefer this method, which is a bit more complicated, but it does help you to get a better visual sense of the position of the south celestial pole.

1 Draw an imaginary line from the star Gacrux at the top of the Southern Cross to Acrux at the bottom of the Cross.
2 Continue that line (from Acrux) and extend it 4.5 times farther; this will place you to a point 4° west of the south celestial pole.
3 Draw an imaginary line that connects Alpha (α) and Beta (β) Centauri, find the midpoint, then draw another imaginary line perpendicular to the previous one, in the direction of the line running down from the Southern Cross. These lines will intersect at a point 4° west of the south celestial pole.
4 Drop your gaze directly down to the horizon, and, once again, you'll be *close* enough to true south to get your general bearings.

Method 3

Here is another way to find south under dark or semi-dark skies.

1 Imagine a line from Gacrux at the top of the Southern Cross to the Alpha (α) star in Musca.
2 Continue that line (from Alpha Musca) and extend it 1.5 times farther; this will place you very close to the south celestial pole.
3 Drop your gaze directly down to the horizon to point very close to true south.

Method 4

The Southern Cross is not always visible from Botswana. But for about half of the year, when the Southern Cross is low or has set, the Magellanic Clouds either are visible or will be visible a few hours after sunset. The south celestial pole makes a near-equilateral triangle with the clouds. Find that imaginary point, then drop your gaze to the horizon to find south.

The south celestial pole

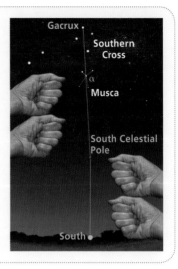

The altitude of the south celestial pole above the horizon is always the same as the latitude of your location on Earth. As the latitude of Maun, Botswana, for instance, is 20° south; the south celestial pole is 20° (two fists) above the horizon. If you live in Gaborone, it's 24°, if in Francistown, 21°. Using Method 3 (see page 57), if you live around Maun or Francistown, you can use your fist to locate the south celestial pole from Alpha (α) Muscae. As one fist held at arm's length covers 10° of sky, and Alpha (α) Muscae is approximately 20° from the south celestial pole, the Pole then lies two fists below Alpha (α) Muscae. Follow the line for two more fists and you will be at the horizon.

Southern stars and wonders

◆ **The False Cross** is not an official constellation but a grouping of stars in a familiar pattern known as an asterism. It resembles the Southern Cross but precedes it in the sky and is slightly larger. The two crosses are separated by about two fists of sky in a rich region of the Milky Way. About midway between the two lies the Eta Carinae Nebula (one of the few nebulae visible to unaided eyes) and the tiny, tight cluster of stars known as the Southern Pleiades, which marks the tip of yet another cross, the Diamond Cross, named for its shape.

Southern Beehive

The Southern Beehive (NGC 2516), a compact open star cluster, lies at the foot of the False Cross. It is visible to unaided eyes as a small fuzzy knot of melded starlight that almost nags the eye. Binoculars will show its 80-odd stars at the core, with a tiny cruciform shape. Light leaving this cluster takes more than 1,000 years to reach our eyes. This month you can compare both the Northern Beehive (M44) and the Southern Beehive on the same night.

The eastern sky at a glance

The long body of Hydra the Female Water Snake lies stretched at its fullest extent and dominates the eastern sky with bright Alphard. The Sail pattern of stars (in the constellation Corvus the Crow), and blue-white, bright Spica (in the constellation of Virgo) are the prime wonders in the low eastern sky, though you may need an unobstructed horizon to see them well. Use Spica to guide you to the snake's tail. Denebola (the tail star of Leo the Lion) shines about three fist-widths to the left of the Sail, with the Sickle of Leo to its north.

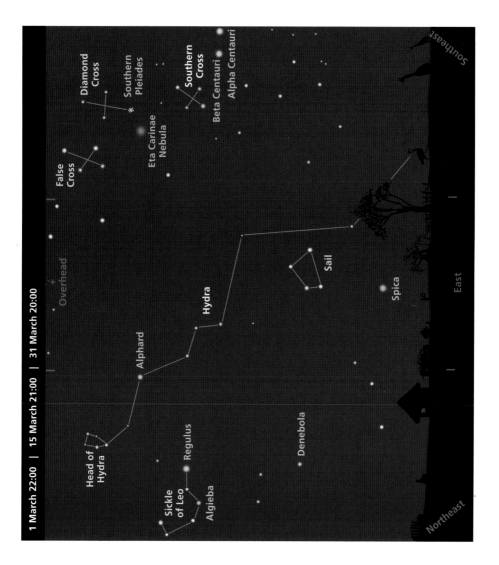

The western sky at a glance

The leading edge of the giant hexagon is heading for the western horizon. Menkar in the head of Cetus the Sea Monster is ready to set due west, and will be followed soon after by the Pleiades star cluster. Canopus shines brightly with its pale yellow light in the southern sky. The giant hexagon of seven bright stars dominates the mid-western sky. The huge formation surrounds rosy-coloured Betelgeuse near its centre. The Pleiades star cluster seems to be dragging the entire ensemble towards the abyss of the western horizon.

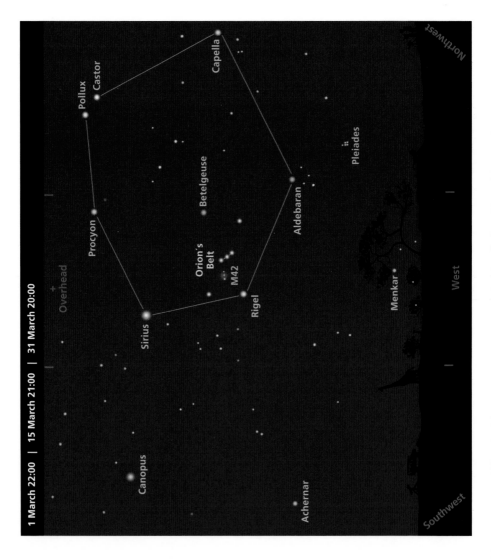

1 March 22:00 | 15 March 21:00 | 31 March 20:00

The northern sky at a glance

Leo the Lion, seen upside down from Botswana, is now at its best for viewing. The lion's mane is also called the Sickle of Leo, with Regulus marking the bottom of the Sickle's handle. Denebola, which marks the Lion's tail, follows Regulus by about two fists away to the east. The Lion is flanked to the west by the Head of Hydra and the Beehive star cluster, and to the east by Berenice's Hair. Sirius, Procyon, Castor and Pollux march steadily closer to the northwestern horizon. Meanwhile, two new beacons have appeared in the eastern sky: blue-white Spica and golden Arcturus. The Big Dipper is now fully in view (upside down), with its bowl spilling its celestial waters onto the thirsty Earth.

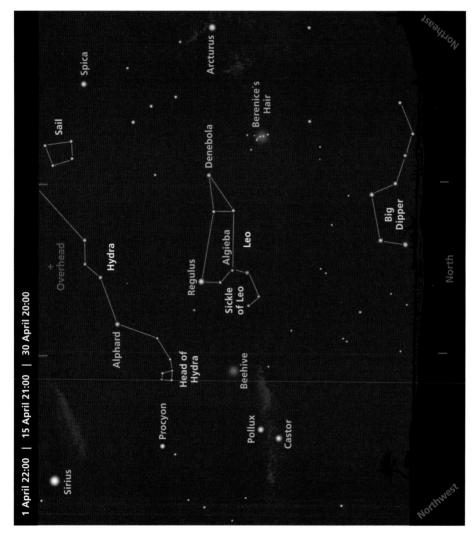

Northern stars and wonders

◆ **Regulus** *(REG-you-luss)* is a gentle blue-white gem and means 'the little king'. Ancients believed the star ruled the affairs of heaven and was a portent of good fortune. The great power bestowed upon this star was probably related to the fact that it reigns highest after sunset during the onset of the northern hemisphere's spring, when life returns to the Earth after winter. In Botswana, this time marks the end of the hot-wet season. Ancients also knew Regulus as Cor Leonis, 'heart of the lion'.

Leo the Lion, with blue-white Regulus visible at the 'heart of the lion' and golden Algieba visible in the 'mane'.

This blue-hot star is 150 times brighter than the Sun and is relatively nearby – its light takes only 79 years to reach our eyes. Leo lies in the path of the Sun, Moon and planets and is regularly visited by them. Regulus marks the position of the Sun every 20 August – just three days prior to when the Sun leaves the astrological house of Leo and slips into Virgo. Occasionally, the Moon will pass directly in front of Regulus and briefly hide it from view; such an occultation (cutting off from view) proves that the Moon is closer to us than the stars. The word 'occultation' derives from the same root word as 'occult' (meaning 'a hidden power').

◆ **Algieba** *(al-GEE-bah)* is a striking golden star in the lion's mane. Its name means 'the forehead', but that appears to be an error. Algieba is an orange giant star, nearly 300 times brighter than our Sun, and 130 light years distant. Although it appears as a single star to the unaided eye, it moves through space with a smaller companion star that is invisible to the naked eye. Algieba also has a giant planet orbiting it which is ten times more massive than our solar system's largest planet (Jupiter).

◆ **Denebola** *(den-EBB-oh-la)* marks the tuft of hair at the end of the lion's tail and means 'the tail of the lion'. It is also the brightest star in the small triangle that forms the lion's hindquarters. The white star is only slightly larger than our Sun and is very close to Earth – its light taking only 36 years to reach our eyes.

◆ **Ursa Major and the Big Dipper** The Big Dipper is a familiar star pattern (asterism) within the larger constellation called Ursa Major, or the Great Bear. The Dipper appears conspicuous because its five middle stars belong to a star cluster – the nearest one to Earth. Note that the second star in from the tip of the Dipper's handle is two stars close together. Both can be seen without optical aid, and are a fun test for naked-eye vision. Actually, anyone with average eyesight should be able to see them. The two stars at the far end of the bowl are the Pointer Stars; they direct travellers to the north, just as the long axis of the Southern Cross can also be used to guide people southward.

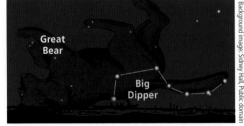

The Big Dipper in the Great Bear is seen upside down in the southern hemisphere.

The southern sky at a glance

The three crosses are at their best for viewing as a trio. The False Cross (with its Southern Beehive cluster) and Southern Cross guard the Eta Carinae Nebula and the Southern Pleiades star cluster, which marks the top of the Diamond Cross. Canopus precedes these wonders in the southwestern sky, shining like a guiding light (be sure to turn the chart to the right to see the correct orientation). The Large Magellanic Cloud has sunk lower in the southwest, while the Southern Triangle and the Pointer Stars to the Southern Cross (Alpha and Beta Centauri) dominate the southeastern domain.

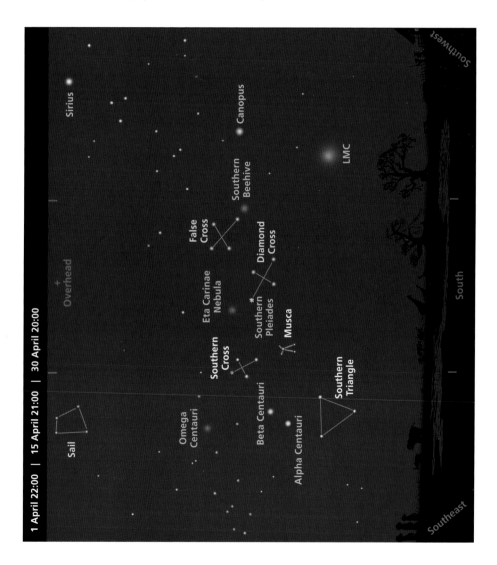

Southern stars and wonders

◆ **Eta Carinae** *(ATE-ah car-E-knee)* **(star and nebula)** A conspicuous, naked-eye nebula surrounds Eta Carinae star, which shines very dimly to the unaided eye because it is very distant; its light takes about 7,500 years to reach our eyes. Nevertheless, it is one of the most incredible stars visible without optical aid. Eta Carinae is a hypergiant star, 150 times more massive than our Sun. It shines about three million times more brightly than the Sun, making it one of the most massive and luminous stars known.

Despite its high mass, astronomers are uncertain of the size of Eta Carinae. It may rival a red giant star like Betelgeuse or Antares, though it is probably much smaller, as depicted in the diagram below.

The star Eta Carinae lies within the Eta Carinae Nebula, a stellar nursery where new stars are being born.

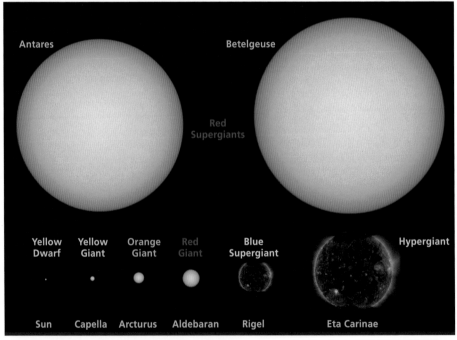

This composite of NASA Sun images illustrates the different kinds of stars described in this book. The images have been scaled to illustrate the rough size of each star compared with our Sun (at lower left).

Eta Carinae's light varies in brightness due to violent outbursts that can cause the star to swell so magnificently that it can rival the brightest stars in the night sky before dimming again. The last time this happened was in 1841, but it could happen again at any time. Eta Carinae is on its deathbed and on the verge of exploding.

The Hubble Space Telescope image of Eta Carinae shows that the star we see with our eyes is actually twin shells of dust and gas, expanding away from the star – the white spot at the centre. These shells were ejected during the nineteenth century's violent outburst.

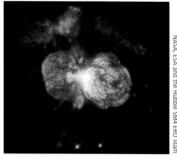

NASA, ESA and the Hubble SM4 ERO Team

When you see the 'star' Eta Carinae, you are actually seeing a tiny nebula within a larger nebula.

Eta Carinae Nebula and the Southern Pleiades Cluster

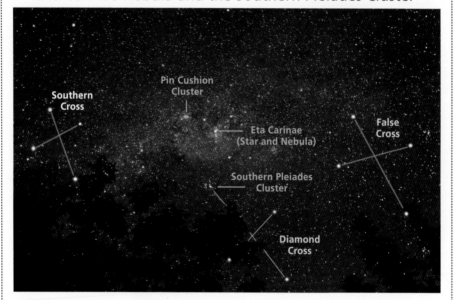

This photograph shows the Eta Carinae Nebula and the Southern Pleiades open star cluster dominating the southern skies. One green line points to the magnificent 'superstar', the hypergiant Eta Carinae, which can be seen faintly with unaided eyes, surrounded by nebulosity. Also shown are two open star clusters: the tiny Pin Cushion, which is best viewed through binoculars, and the Southern Pleiades, which is much larger but is also visible to unaided eyes. Note, too, how the Milky Way washes through this region of sky in delicate folds.

You'll find the Eta Carinae Nebula about midway between the Southern Cross and False Cross, appearing as a misty patch of light in the Milky Way.

The Pin Cushion cluster is an open star cluster.

◆ **Pin Cushion cluster** (NGC 3532) Anyone looking at the Eta Carinae Nebula and its hypergiant through binoculars will get an extra treat – a view of the Pin Cushion open star cluster in the same field of view. The cluster is visible to the unaided eye under dark skies as a tiny knot of diffuse light, but binoculars will show it as an ellipse of prickly starlight. The view is reminiscent of a cushion in which one stores pins and needles.

◆ **Southern Pleiades** *(PLEE-uh-deez)* **IC 2602** is a family of stars about three finger-widths south of Eta Carinae. It looks like a fuzzy sprinkling of starlight at the top of the Diamond Cross. With an averted gaze, it has the shape of a little doll. It's called the Southern Pleiades to differentiate it from the more brilliant Pleiades star cluster in the north (described in January).

◆ **NGC 3114** is another naked-eye open star cluster in the vicinity of the Eta Carinae Nebula. The light from this cluster takes about 3,000 years to reach our eyes. The cluster is best viewed through binoculars.

The region around the Eta Carinae Nebula is rich with stars and open star clusters.

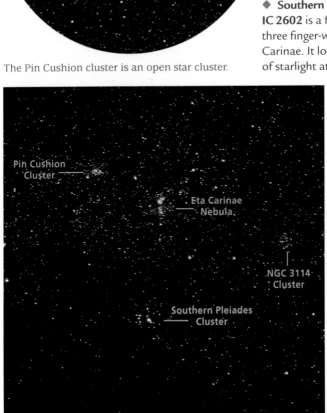

The eastern sky at a glance

Stars of Hydra the Female Water Snake, the Sail pattern (of Corvus the Crow) and the blue-white Spica (in Virgo the Virgin) dominate the view midway up the sky. Golden Arcturus has risen to become the beacon of the low northeastern sky, while red Antares burns even lower in the southeastern sky, and a clear, unobstructed horizon is needed to see it well. Between them are the balance stars of Libra: Zubenelgenubi and Zubeneschamali. These unusual names have their origins in Arabic and are described in June.

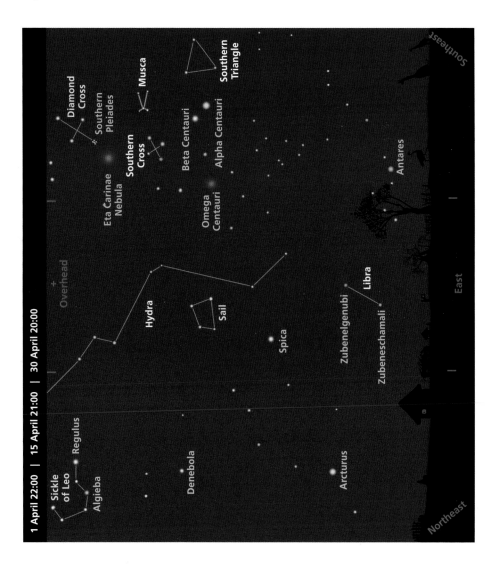

Virgo

Next to Hydra, Virgo is the second-largest constellation, and was one of the first constellations to receive a name. Many cultures imagined its stars as a virgin: the Romans associated Virgo with the goddess Ceres who descended to Earth to preside over the harvest. Early Christians claimed it

Spica and the harvest season

Virgo's brightest star is Spica. To some of Botswana's indigenous people, it is known as *Magakgala*. When rising, Spica told the people it was time to harvest their maize. The association is interesting, especially given that Virgo is classically seen as a goddess of the harvest and is often depicted with an ear of corn (maize) in her hand.

represented the Virgin Mary ascending to heaven. Astronomically, the ascension occurs not in April but in August, when the Sun enters Virgo. It is then that the Catholics celebrate the Feast of the Assumption, or the reunion of the Virgin with her Son.

Virgo's brightest star is Spica, a hot-blue star that is 14 times larger and 12,000 times more luminous than our Sun. Light leaving its surface takes 250 light years to reach our eyes. Virgo is the seventh and largest constellation of the zodiac.

Spica

Jupiter

It is not unusual to see the Moon or planets occasionally visiting the constellation of Virgo at night, as Jupiter did in 2017, when it was seen close to Spica.

The western sky at a glance

Orion is poised for setting in the west. Brilliant Sirius dominates the mid-western sky, with Procyon and the Twin stars (Castor and Pollux) arcing away from it towards the northwestern horizon. Canopus shines brightly in the mid-southwestern sky, together with the False Cross. The Sickle of Leo reigns in the mid-northern skies, with Alphard, the Head of Hydra and the Beehive cluster sailing closer to the west.

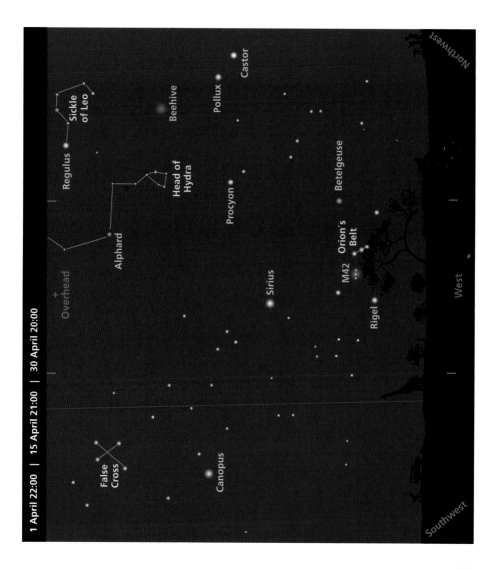

The northern sky at a glance

The large, visually delicate star cluster known as Berenice's Hair has taken dominion over the mid-northern skies. Hydra the Female Water Snake (with Alphard) and Leo the Lion have moved farther to the west, with Leo's tail star, Denebola, almost brushing Berenice's Hair. The stellar diamond Spica in Virgo the Virgin has moved closer to centre stage; Arcturus is not far behind. The Sail of Corvus the Crow lies directly overhead. Low in the north, the Great Bear's belly is slipping away from the centre. The Great Bear's head has already set, but its paw prints can still be seen. The Northern Crown is coming into view in the northeast, while Zubenelgenubi and Zubeneschamali are midway in the eastern sky.

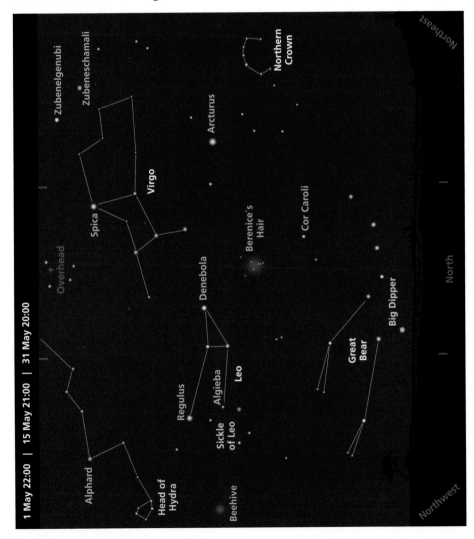

Northern stars and wonders

◆ **Corvus the Crow** appears as a trapezoid of four conspicuous stars (called the Sail) near Spica. Look carefully at its lower right star, as it is a naked-eye double star – a chance alignment of two stars lying along the same line of sight. The constellation is named after the crow that the Greek god, Apollo, sent to fetch some water in a cup. According to legend, the crow got distracted and lied to Apollo about why he returned so late. As punishment for lying, Apollo condemned the crow to eternal thirst both on Earth and in the heavens.

◆ **Coma Berenices** *(CO-ma Bare-uh-NYE-sees)* or **Berenice's Hair** is both a constellation and an open star cluster. Look for seven prominent stars in a Y-shaped pattern – with twice that many fainter, naked-eye stars glittering like dew on a cobweb. This Y-shaped core also marks the heart of the Coma Berenices star cluster. Like the Big Dipper, it appears so large in the sky because the cluster is so close. Its light takes less than 300 years to reach our eyes.

Background image: Sidney Hall, Public domain

Berenice's Hair is a constellation and an open star cluster. Look out for the Y-shaped pattern formed by seven stars.

Ancient cultures throughout time have envisioned the star group as locks of hair in the heavens. The earliest legends come from Egypt at the top of Africa, where they were seen as the beautiful amber locks of Queen Berenice II who swore to cut them off if her husband returned safely from war. When he did, she kept her vow and placed her hair in the Temple of Aphrodite (the goddess of beauty). When someone stole the hair from the temple, a court astronomer told the king that it had been placed in the heavens by the gods for all to see and admire.

Three leaps of the impala

The early people of Africa shared star lore through oral traditions. Migrating tribes carried the tales of their homelands with them, until they abandoned the old and adopted the new, creating personal tales that better fitted their relationship with their new environment. In the Arabian Peninsula, for instance, the three pairs of stars that mark three paws of Ursa Major (the Great Bear) were seen as the hoof prints of a gazelle making three leaps away from a misty waterhole or lake (which is how they imagined Berenice's Hair).

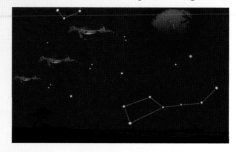

Berenice's Hair and the three pairs of stars close by may be imagined as a waterhole with three leaping impala leaving their hoofprints close by.

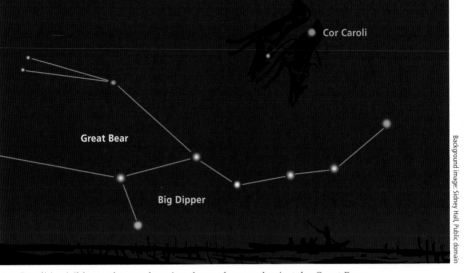

Background image: Sidney Hall, Public domain

Cor Caroli is visible on the two hunting dogs who are chasing the Great Bear.

◆ **Cor Caroli** *(CORE Ka-ROLL-ee)* is the brightest star of a small constellation known as **Canes Venatici** *(KAN-es veh-NAT-ih-see)* – the two hunting dogs of **Boötes** *(boh-OH-tease)* the Herder. Cor Caroli is the brighter of the two dogs. When seen from the northern hemisphere, the dogs chase the Great Bear endlessly around the North Star. From Botswana, we cannot see the North Star, so we see only a part of that chase.

The name Cor Caroli means 'the heart of Charles' and refers to Charles I of England who was beheaded in 1649 for treason. Although we see Cor Caroli shining as one star to the unaided eye, it is actually a double star, whose light takes 110 years to reach our eyes.

Herding cattle

In some early African cultures, the Big Dipper was viewed as an animal being herded into an enclosure; in early American societies, it represented a bear being followed by three people.

Since the bowl of the Big Dipper is widely seen as the body of an animal and its tail stars as three people, it is not surprising then that indigenous legends, such as those told by the Tswana, frame the Dipper's Bowl as a Cow and the three tail stars as young herders. In this interpretation, Cor Caroli and its companion are the herders' dogs.

A contemporary interpretation of Cor Caroli as herders' dogs, while the Big Dipper is being herded into an enclosure.

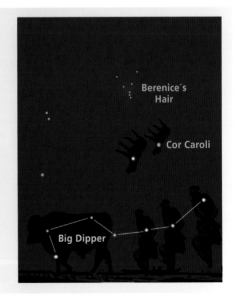

The southern sky at a glance

The False Cross and Diamond Cross have moved away from the southern meridian (the imaginary line in the sky defining north–south). Now the Southern Cross has moved into that prime position – with tiny Musca the Fly beneath it and Centaurus the Centaur arching above it. The Eta Carinae Nebula and the Southern Pleiades star cluster are still prominently placed above the southern horizon. Canopus precedes these wonders in the southwestern sky. The Southern Triangle and the Pointer Stars to the Southern Cross (Alpha and Beta Centauri) dominate the southeastern region of the sky. (They will be discussed next month.) The Sail of Corvus the Crow and the tail of Hydra the Female Water Snake are high overhead.

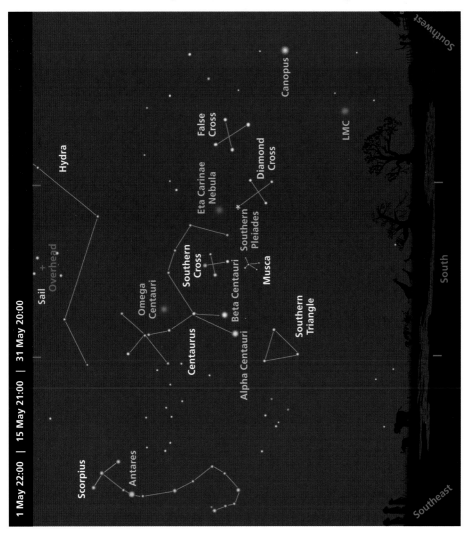

Animals in the stars

The indigenous people of Botswana saw many animals among the stars. Those in and around the Southern Cross and Coalsack are among the best known. Early Basarwa tradition tells us the four bright stars of the Southern Cross were known as *Dithutlwa*, which means 'the giraffes'. The brightest two are males and the fainter two are females.

In the far western Kalahari, Botswana's indigenous people saw the dark Coalsack Nebula just as early European explorers did – as an 'old bag of the night'.

A Botswana stamp depicts the four bright stars of the Southern Cross, seen at left on the stamp, as giraffes.

Coalsack (Insterstellar dust cloud)

Earth Clouds

◆ **Coalsack Nebula** Look just a little southeast of the Southern Cross for a black, pear-shaped void in the Milky Way. Early southern explorers called it the Coalsack because it looked like a sooty sack used to carry coal.

The Coalsack is actually a cold, dark cloud of dust and gas (dark nebula) seen silhouetted against the rich stars of the Milky Way – just as earthly clouds look dark at night when seen against the starlit sky away from city lights. The lightless patch of the Coalsack is much more distant: we see this inky cloud some 600 light years away. Typical clouds in the atmosphere above Earth are only a few thousand metres away.

The Coalsack Nebula was so named because it looked like a sooty sack used to carry coal.

Constellations of darkness

Dark clouds like the Coalsack are part of a family of dark constellations. Look for the Dark Giraffe, comprised of dark clouds that line the Milky Way: the Coalsack is the Giraffe's head, while a long stretch of darkness starting at Beta Centauri and leading to the Scorpion's Tail is the animal's neck and torso. Other fainter dark clouds form the legs.

Left: When the Dark Giraffe rises in May and early June shortly after sunset, its head and neck are upright.
Below: The full length of the Dark Giraffe is visible – from the Coalsack (the kite-shaped dark patch in the upper right corner), through Alpha and Beta Centauri (the two bright stars at upper right) and straight to the dark clouds in the Milky Way next to the Scorpion's Tail (near the centre of the photo).

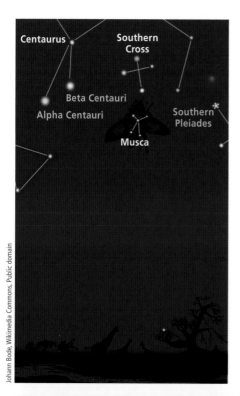

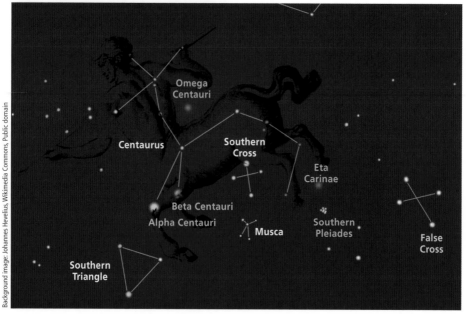

◆ **Musca the Fly** This tiny but conspicuous constellation lies just below the foot of the Southern Cross. It was introduced to astronomy in the sixteenth century by Dutch navigators, some of whom knew it as Apis the Bee. Either way, the constellation celebrates the insect kingdom, which is relatively poorly represented in the night sky.

◆ **Centaurus** is a vast constellation. It depicts the Centaur – a mythical beast that is half human, half animal. In Greek legend, it was the scholarly centaur known as Chiron that taught many Greek gods and heroes. Chiron was placed in the sky after Hercules accidentally shot him with a poisoned arrow.

Left: Musca the Fly can be seen just below the Southern Cross.

Below: The vast constellation of Centaurus is comprised of many stars and appears to leap over the Southern Cross.

European Southern Observatory

Omega Centauri is an ancient globular cluster shining with the light of over a million stars.

◆ **Omega Centauri** To the unaided eye, Omega Centauri appears as a faint star that doesn't quite look right. If you use averted vision, it will appear to swell a bit, while the surrounding stars remain as pinpoints of light. That is because Omega Centauri is not a star at all but the most magnificent example of a globular star cluster. It shines with the light of a million stars all packed together in a globular mass some 17,000 light years distant in the far reaches of our galaxy. Omega Centauri is almost as old as the universe itself. Astronomers now believe that this object comprises the core remains of a dwarf galaxy (like the Magellanic Clouds) that our Milky Way galaxy swallowed long ago.

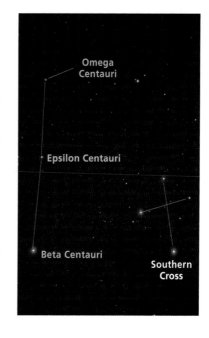

Find Omega Centauri by drawing an imaginary line from Beta Centauri through Epsilon Centauri. Continue in the same direction until you see a fainter fuzzy object: Omega Centauri.

The eastern sky at a glance

The two brightest stars of Libra the Scales – Zubenelgenubi and Zubeneschamali – grace the mid-eastern sky, but these are discussed in more detail in June, when they are at their highest. Blue-white Spica (in Virgo the Virgin) has climbed to a lofty perch. Golden Arcturus and the Northern Crown dominate the mid-northeastern sky, while low in the east-southeast, Antares burns prominently at the heart of Scorpius the Scorpion, whose tail nearly stings the naked-eye star clusters M6 and M7. The Teapot of Sagittarius and the Salt Shaker of Ophiuchus are on the rise as well, but you may need a clear horizon to see them.

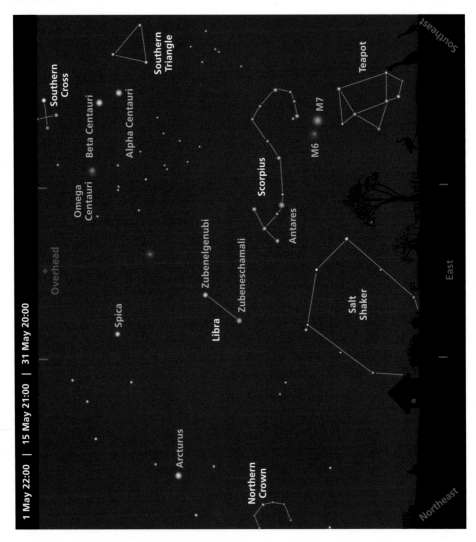

The western sky at a glance

A triangle of bright stars (Alphard, Procyon and Sirius) graces the western sky, with Sirius and Procyon almost neck and neck as they near the horizon before setting. Castor and Pollux join the race farther to the northwest. Hydra is snaking down, head first, towards the western horizon. Regulus in the Sickle of Leo is higher up in the northwest. Two familiar star patterns – the False Cross and the Southern Cross – are high in the southern sky, while yellow Canopus rules the low southwestern sky.

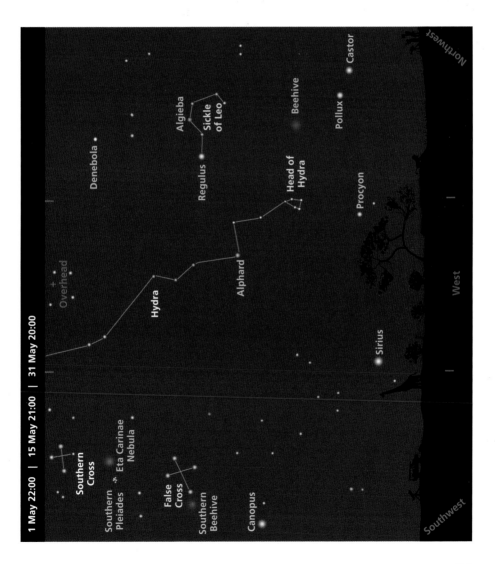

The northern sky at a glance

Arcturus in Boötes the Herdsman rules the mid-northern skies. Its golden light shines down upon the welcoming Earth. Preceding it, and nearly overhead, is blue-white Spica, followed by the two inconspicuous stars in the zodiacal constellation Libra, Zubeneschamali and Zubenelgenubi. Trailing Arcturus in the northeast we find the delicate Northern Crown with its stellar gem, Alphecca. The Big Dipper has already begun to sink beneath the northwestern horizon, while two new star patterns – the Keystone of Hercules and the Head of Draco the Dragon – are rising in the northeast ahead of crystalline Vega and ruddy Rasalhague.

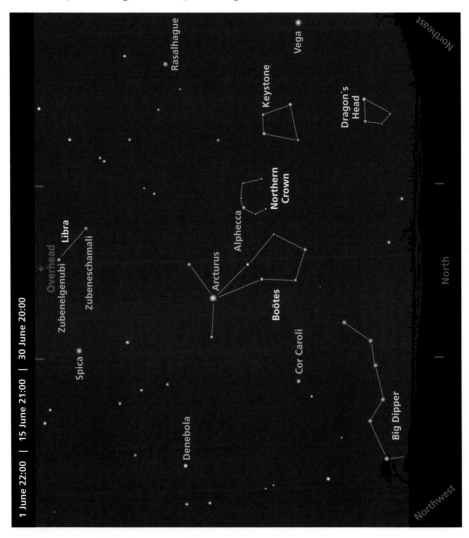

Northern stars and wonders

◆ **Arcturus** *(ark-TOUR-us)* is the third brightest star in the night sky and one of the most splendid. It is the only star mentioned in the Bible, and early Christian skywatchers saw Arcturus as the Great Shepherd and Harvester of Souls. Its name means 'clamorous' or 'noisy' – descriptive of the shouts that shepherds make when driving their flocks. Boötes the Herdsman, in which Arcturus lies, is one of those noisy shepherds. An orange giant star, 25 times larger than our Sun, Arcturus is also relatively close to Earth – its light takes only 37 years to reach our eyes.

To find Arcturus, find the handle of the Big Dipper then use your eyes to continue moving in an arc shape up to Arcturus, about three fist-widths away.

American astronomers used their powerful telescopes to harvest the light of Arcturus to turn on the lights at the start of the 1933 World's Fair held in Chicago, USA.

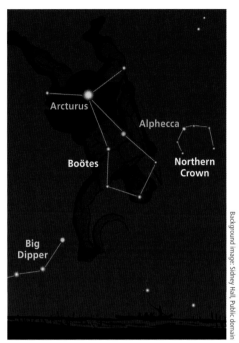

Background image: Sidney Hall, Public domain

Arcturus, the third brightest star in the sky, lies in Boötes the Herdsman.

Arcturus, the morning star

To Botswana's indigenous people, Arcturus (the brightest star in the photo), like Sirius, was known as *Kgogamasigo*, which means 'morning star'. Rising around 4:00 in November – the ploughing season – Arcturus reminded people to feed and water their oxen well, so that maximum use could be made of them during the long daylight hours.

Arcturus is the brightest star in the entire northern hemisphere of stars, and Sirius the brightest in the entire southern hemisphere. On page 41, we introduced Sirius as 'the leader', who pulls the southern stars across the night sky from left to right (facing south); conversely Arcturus pulls the northern stars across the night sky from right to left (facing north).

Arcturus was known as *Kgogamasigo* ('morning star') by Botswana's indigenous people.

Corona Borealis as a trance dance

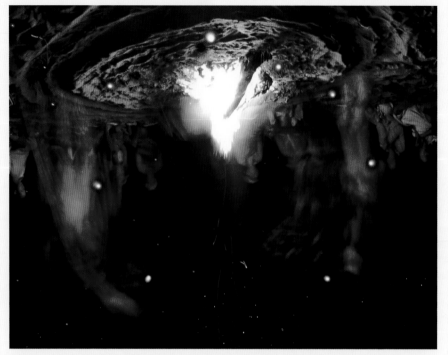

Although we see it 'upside down', the broken circlet of stars that forms Corona Borealis can easily be imagined as people performing a trance dance around a fire, with Alphecca being the fire and the other stars people dancing around it.

◆ **Alphecca** *(al-FECK-ah)* is the brightest star in the Northern Crown star pattern (Corona Borealis is the official name of the constellation). Alphecca means 'the pearl of the crown'; it is also popularly known as Gemma – derived from the Latin word meaning 'gem' or 'jewel', making Gemma the jewel in the Northern Crown. Alphecca has also been translated as 'the bright one of the dish', referring to the star pattern's resemblance to a broken plate. Alphecca is a white-hot star, six times larger and 70 times more luminous than our Sun. Light leaving the star takes 75 years to reach our eyes.

◆ **Zubenelgenubi** *(Zoo-BEN-el-je-NEW-bee)* and **Zubeneschamali** *(Zoo-BEN-ess-sha-MAH-lee),* meaning 'the southern claw' and 'the northern claw' respectively, are the two brightest stars in the zodiacal constellation of Libra the Scales. They used to mark the position of Scorpius the Scorpion's claws – until they were separated from that constellation to form part of Libra. Zubeneschamali is the only green star visible to the unaided eyes. These two stars were also known as the Balance stars because, more than 2,000 years ago, the Sun was in Libra when people experienced autumn equinox (a time of equal day and night) in the northern hemisphere.

The Earth wobbles on its axis very slowly, like a slowly turning top, causing our view of the Sun to appear to move westward against the stars ever so slightly every year. This slight movement adds up over time. So, about every 2,000 years, we see the Sun slip westward into the preceding zodiacal constellation. Today, for instance, the autumn equinox in the northern hemisphere occurs with the Sun in Virgo, the constellation that precedes Libra.

◆ **Libra the Scales** Libra is the only classical constellation that appears not to have its origins in Mesopotamia. Arab and Greek skywatchers imagined these stars as the claws of Scorpius the Scorpion. Then, around the time of Julius Caesar's reign (46–44 BCE),

Did you know?

Animated Libra
In ancient Persia (now Iran), skywatchers envisioned Libra the Scales as a man or woman who lifts the scales in one hand, and grasps a lamb with the other, with the lamb serving as the ancient weight. In divine interpretations, these scales determined the wages of sin and the price of redemption. Had this interpretation stuck, Libra would not have been the only inanimate object in the zodiac.

the Romans conceived of the claws as part of Libra, a new constellation that depicted Julius Caesar holding a pair of scales. In time, the Emperor was removed from the sky, leaving only the scales behind. Libra is the only constellation of the zodiac that represents an inanimate object.

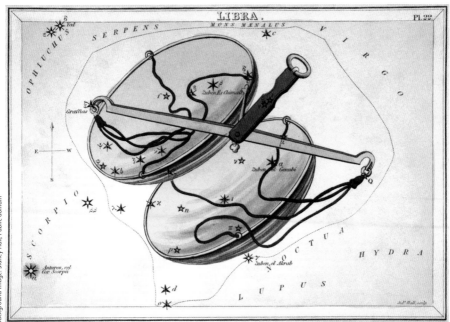

Background image: Sidney Hall, Public domain

Libra the Scales as depicted in *Urania's Mirror*, circa 1825. Note how the positions of Zubeneschamali and Zubenelgenubi (spelled 'Zuben Es Chimali' and 'Zuben el Genubi' on this card) mark the positions of the scales.

The southern sky at a glance

Alpha and Beta Centauri dominate the mid-southern skies, pointing westward towards the Southern Cross. The Southern Triangle is now approaching its highest point in the south, above which shines an array of bluish stars in the rich Milky Way, west of the Scorpion, in Lupus the Wolf. The Sail of Corvus and Omega Centauri have slipped away from their highest points and are now drifting towards the west and southwest, respectively. In the southwestern sky, Canopus is near setting and will be followed shortly by the False Cross. Blue Peacock has risen to a comfortable height in the southeastern sky, which is dominated by the Teapot of Sagittarius star pattern and the very heart of the Milky Way.

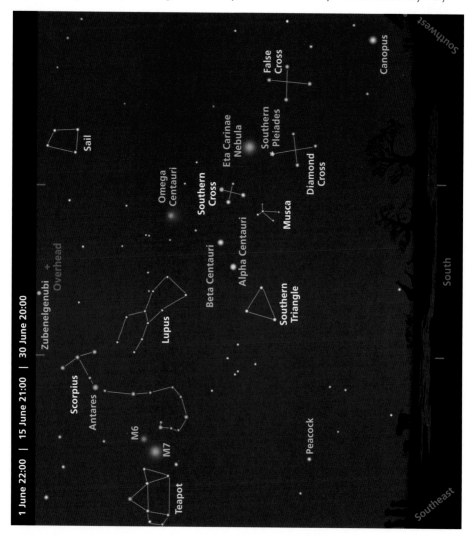

Southern stars and wonders

Alpha and Beta Centauri are two bright stars that point to the Southern Cross like a finger. Together they are often referred to as the Pointer Stars; as such, they are among the most famous stars in the sky.

Alpha and Beta Centauri, the Pointer Stars, so named because they point to the Southern Cross.

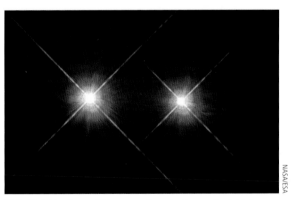

This Hubble Space Telescope image shows that Alpha Centauri is a multiple star.

NASA/ESA

◆ **Alpha Centauri** *(AL-fah sen-TOR-ee)* is the closest star to the Earth visible to the unaided eye. It is also a multiple star – though you cannot see it with unaided eyes. The system consists of two equally bright stars orbiting one another with another very dim companion, Proxima Centauri, which is just a little bit closer to us than the brighter pair. When light leaves the Alpha Centauri system (at a speed of 300,000 kilometres per second), it takes about four years to reach our eyes. Alpha Centauri is also the fourth brightest star in the sky.

◆ **Beta Centauri** *(BEY-tah sen-TOR-ee)* looks as if it's a close companion to Alpha Centauri, therefore it too must be close to Earth ... but this is only an illusion. In reality, Beta Centauri is about 20 times larger than Alpha Centauri and 90 times farther away. Like Alpha Centauri, it is also a triple star system.

Pointer Star lore

The Southern Cross with its Pointer Stars (Alpha and Beta Centauri) is well known in Botswana lore.

A pride of lions

Some indigenous people of the Kalahari envisioned the Pointer Stars as a pride of lions. The pointers to the Southern Cross were formerly men who became lions. They were turned into stars because girls liked to look at them. The nineteenth-century linguist, Wilhelm Bleek, wrote that the meaning behind this myth remains unclear. (See page 113.) These lions now lie not far from three lionesses (the three brightest stars of the Southern Cross), who protect a cub (the faintest star of the Southern Cross).

The Southern Cross, with Alpha and Beta Centauri, has been interpreted as a pride of lions.

The four giraffes of the Southern Cross

The four stars of the Southern Cross were seen as *Dithutlwa* (giraffes), described on page 74. In northern Botswana, the indigenous people also added Alpha and Beta Centauri to this tower of giraffes. Throughout Botswana, different tribes had different interpretations of which ones were male and female.

The Southern Cross seen as *Dithutlwa*, the giraffes. In northern Botswana, Alpha and Beta Centauri were added to this giraffe tower.

A lone giraffe

The lofty name *Dithutlwa* (giraffes) suggests the stars are rising above the trees. Seen in another way, Alpha and Beta Centauri are the neck of a single giraffe and the Southern Cross is the giraffe's head, which is visible when these stars are rising.

The Southern Cross viewed as the head of a single giraffe, with Alpha and Beta Centauri as the neck.

Lupus the Wolf

The splash of bluish stars above the Milky Way (in the region of Alpha and Beta Centauri and the Southern Cross) makes up the star pattern known as Lupus the Wolf. The dark cloud to the lower left of the Southern Cross is the famous Coalsack dark nebula (detailed description on page 74).

Lupus the Wolf howls above the Milky Way.

Lupus the Leopard

It's not inconceivable that some indigenous people in Botswana could have imagined the brightest stars of Lupus – seen between the Scorpion (to the left in the image at right) and the Pointer Stars (right of centre) – as a leopard, or perhaps a lioness. North African tribes imagined them in this way. Others may have shared the same view. To some early Arabs, for instance, Lupus was *Al Fhad* (the leopard), and to others it was *Al Sadah* (the lioness).

Lupus the Leopard prowls above the Milky Way.

The eastern sky at a glance

Lupus the Wolf, Scorpius and the Teapot of Sagittarius are the most prominent star patterns in the southeastern sky. Zubeneschamali and Zubenelgenubi (the scale stars of Libra) lead them across the sky. Golden Arcturus reigns supreme in the northern sky, followed by the gentle arc of stars of the Northern Crown. The bright white star, Altair, is just rising above the eastern horizon. (You will need a clear, unobstructed horizon to see it.) Rasalhague, the brightest star in the Salt Shaker of Ophiuchus the Serpent Bearer, is the most prominent star in the mid-northeastern heavens.

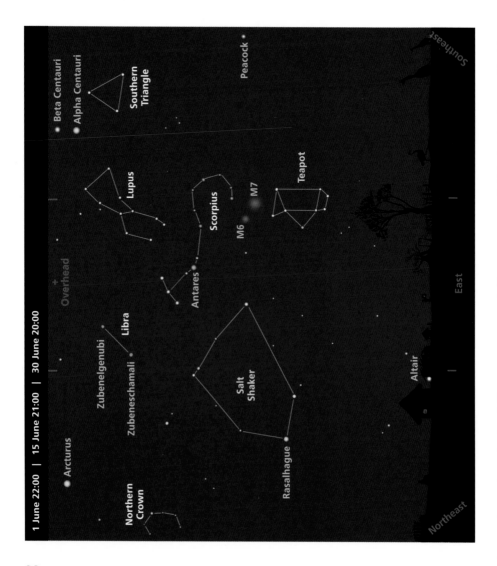

The western sky at a glance

Hydra the Female Water Snake has sunk head first into the western horizon. Regulus (in the Sickle of Leo the Lion) and Alphard (in Hydra) are almost neck and neck in their race towards setting – followed by another race between Denebola (the Lion's tail star) in the northwest and the False Cross in the southwest. Spica (in Virgo) and the Sail of Corvus dominate the high western view.

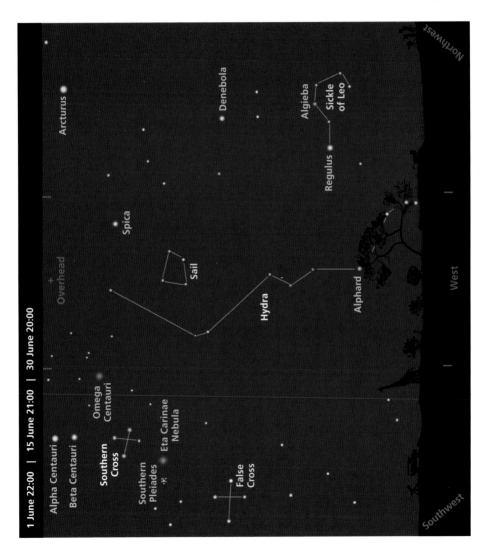

The northern sky at a glance

The high northern sky is dominated by the Salt Shaker figure of Ophiuchus the Serpent Bearer, with ruddy Rasalhague. Three star patterns (the Northern Crown, the Keystone and the Dragon's Head) are noticeable in the low northern sky. Together with golden Arcturus, they form a graceful arc from the mid-northwestern sky to the low north-northeastern sky. Another arc of stars – the handle of the Big Dipper (now low in the northwest) – arcs to Arcturus, then speeds on to Spica (in the mid-western sky). In the northeast, crystalline Vega, blue Deneb and blue Altair form a prominent triangle of three bright stars that measures four fists long and two fists wide. The star pattern of

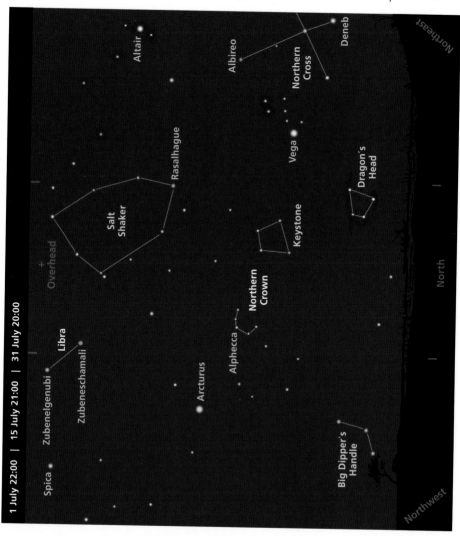

the Northern Cross runs through it, with Albireo marking the foot of the Cross. Look high in the north-northwestern sky for the Balance Stars (Zubenelgenubi and Zubeneschamali in Libra the Scales).

Northern stars and wonders

◆ **The Keystone** is a modest star pattern of four stars covering about a fist-width of sky. Its stars are not tremendously bright, but the pattern is recognizable as a distinct keystone – the central stone at the top of an arch that locks the structure together – midway between the Northern Crown and brilliant Vega.

The great globular cluster M13 in the Keystone.

Hercules the Strongman or Elephants at a waterhole

Ancient stargazers saw Hercules as a strongman among the stars – with the Keystone representing the bottom of his loincloth attire – stepping on the Dragon's Head. In Botswana, we can imagine the Keystone and the Dragon's Head instead as part of a parade of elephants, and the Northern Crown's curve of stars as a waterhole.

Hercules kneels in his loincloth attire while stepping on the Dragon's Head.

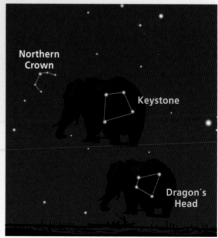

The Keystone and Dragon's Head are imagined as part of a parade of elephants.

The southern sky at a glance

Scorpius the Scorpion, with its striking curved tail and the red giant Antares, dominates the high southern sky. The Milky Way pours through the Scorpion from the neighbouring Teapot of Sagittarius. Between them glow the misty (or we could say steamy) orbs of the open star clusters M6 and M7. The Southern Triangle has reached the apex of its arc across the sky; it seems to be pushing Alpha and Beta Centauri westward off the celestial stage. Between the Southern Triangle and the Tail of the Scorpion are the neglected stars of Ara the Altar, which contains a conspicuous naked-eye pairing of reasonably bright stars. The three crosses (Southern, Diamond and False) are tumbling down towards the southwestern horizon.

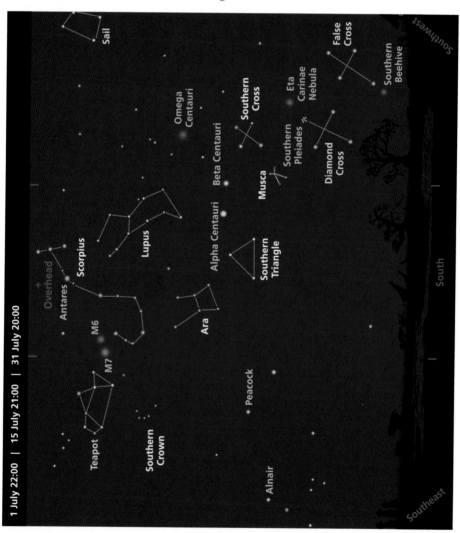

Peacock and Alnair are making their presence known in the southeastern sky, each with their softly glowing blue light. Peacock is in the lead as it marches ever higher into the southern sky.

Southern stars and wonders

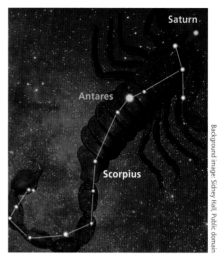

◆ **Antares** *(an-TAR-ease)* is the red pulsing heart of the constellation Scorpius the Scorpion – one of the few constellations in the night sky that actually looks like what it is supposed to represent. Antares burns so red that ancient stargazers called it the 'Rival of Mars' (which is what Antares means) as Mars has long been known as the Red Planet. In Greek mythology, Gaia (Earth Mother), angered by Orion's decision to kill all animals on Earth, called upon Scorpius to kill Orion, which it did by stinging him on the foot. The act attracted the attention of Zeus who honoured Gaia by placing Orion and the Scorpion in opposite parts of the sky, so that when the Scorpion rises, Orion sets, and the two never have to meet again.

Seen from Botswana, the Scorpion marks the highest point in the sky. It is not uncommon to see the Moon and planets visiting the Scorpion, as shown in this June 2015 image with Saturn near the head of Scorpius.

Fire-finishing star

The stunning heart of the Scorpion, reddish Antares, did not go unnoticed by Botswana's indigenous people. Some saw this celestial burning ember as one of their 'Fire-finishing' stars; they had several at different times of the year.

Others may have known Antares as *Magakgala.* When visible in the early evening, possibly along with Spica (which may have also carried the same name), it told them that maize should be harvested.

Whenever Antares rose in the east after sunset, it would set in the west very late at night, by which time the campfires had diminished and the star had vanished into the growing dawn.

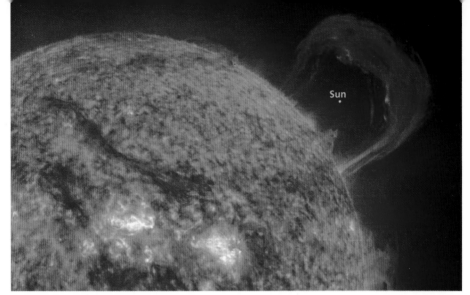

This image depicts the relative size of our Sun to the gigantic star, Antares. A close-up NASA image of our Sun has been significantly enlarged to illustrate the size difference. The image on page 64 shows how the Sun and Antares compare size-wise to other stars in this book.

The Scorpion is in a region of sky rich in dark nebulae that dim the light coming from Antares – a red giant star some 700 times wider than our Sun and shining 10,000 times more brightly than it. And that's through the dust! Sweep the dust clouds away and the star would shine about 10 times more brightly. Antares is an old and dying star whose light pulsates over time (so it can appear slightly brighter or dimmer at different times). Light leaving its surface takes 550 years to reach our eyes.

Dusty clouds deep in space dim the light coming from Antares. A dim, naked-eye, globular star cluster known as M4 lies close by; to see its fuzzy form better, use binoculars.

Tail clusters

The area in and around the Scorpion's Tail harbours some bright star clusters and stellar associations. One object, the False Comet, lies directly in the Tail. To unaided eyes, it looks like a fuzzy comet brushing the sky with its dusty tail. But if you look at this luminous 'comet' with binoculars, you will see that it is not a comet at all but a rich assortment of open star clusters strung out in a line, one after the other. This cluster row is actually a large association of hot young stars that formed together in space in one of our galaxy's spiral arms.

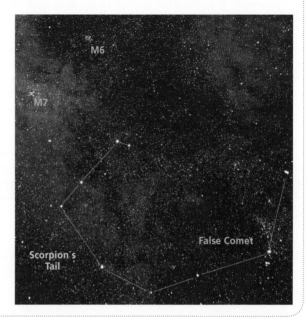

Star clusters around the tail of Scorpius.

Just beyond the tail of Scorpius are two naked-eye open star clusters, M6 and M7. M7 is visible to the unaided eye as a fuzzy ball of light just off the two stinger stars in the Scorpion's Tail. In binoculars, it is a loose sprinkling of about 80 stars. Light from the cluster travels about 1,000 years to reach our eyes.

M6 is a much smaller and more compact cluster, but it is still visible to the unaided eye as a small patch of dim light. M6 also has about 80 stars, but it lies about 600 light years more distant than M7. It appears smaller to us because it is much farther away. Use these two clusters to imagine the true depths of space. So infrequently do we get a chance to compare two similar objects in such close proximity.

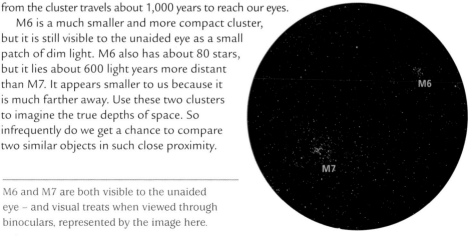

M6 and M7 are both visible to the unaided eye – and visual treats when viewed through binoculars, represented by the image here.

Lion lore

Lion eyes

Can you see the lion in Scorpius? As shown at right, the Scorpion's curved tail can be imagined as the outline of a lion's face, with two pairs of naked-eye stars marking the lion's eyes. Note that the pair of stars on the right is wider apart than the pair on the left, its stars so close together that skywatchers usually need binoculars to see them.

To the Khoikhoi of southern Botswana, the tighter pair alone was known as the 'Eyes of the Lion'.

Lioness and cubs on the hunt

Botswana's indigenous people saw the reddish star (Betelgeuse) in Orion as a lion. It is possible that other reddish stars (such as Antares) were also imagined as lions.

Two pairs of stars in the tail of Scorpius may be seen as the eyes of a lion.

Consistent with Botswanan folklore, Antares and its two attendant stars can be imagined as a lioness with her two cubs, and the three brightest stars in the head of Scorpius as their prey – in this case, Cape Buffalo.

The eastern sky at a glance

The Scorpion and the Teapot of Sagittarius are the most prominent star patterns in the high eastern sky. The Paper Boat of Capricornus is just rising. Peacock is the brightest star in the southeastern sky; it is also the highest of three fairly bright stars in a curved row, the other two being Alnair and Fomalhaut, the latter rising just above the horizon. Altair and Vega dominate the mid-northeastern sky. They form a noticeable triangle with Rasalhague, which is now moving towards its highest position in the north.

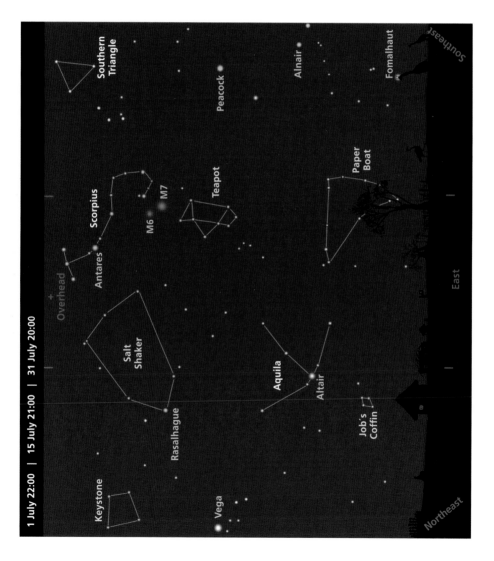

The western sky at a glance

Spica in Virgo the Virgin and the Sail of Corvus are well placed in the mid-western sky. Denebola in the tail of Leo the Lion is near setting. Golden Arcturus is the most prominent star in the northwestern sky, flanked by the delicate Northern Crown. Alpha and Beta Centauri are still high in the southern sky, while the Southern Cross is starting its descent towards the horizon. Red Antares in Scorpius rules the sky overhead.

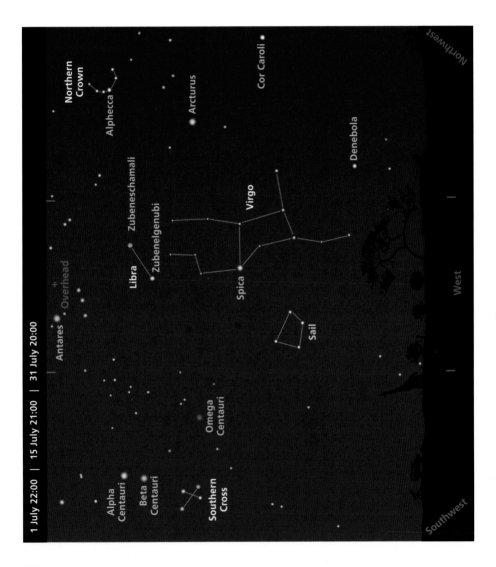

The northern sky at a glance

The graceful arc of patterned starlight mentioned in July (made up of the Northern Crown, the Keystone of Hercules and the Dragon's Head), led by Arcturus, is still noticeable in the northern sky, although the entire view has shifted towards the northwest, where Arcturus is heading for setting. In the northeast, crystalline Vega, blue Deneb and blue-white Altair form a prominent triangle of three bright stars that measures four fists long and two fists wide. The Northern Cross runs through it, with Albireo marking the foot of the Cross. Vega, the brightest of the three, is nearing its highest point in the sky as seen from Botswana, while Rasalhague in the Salt Shaker pattern of Ophiuchus has just moved off its lofty position.

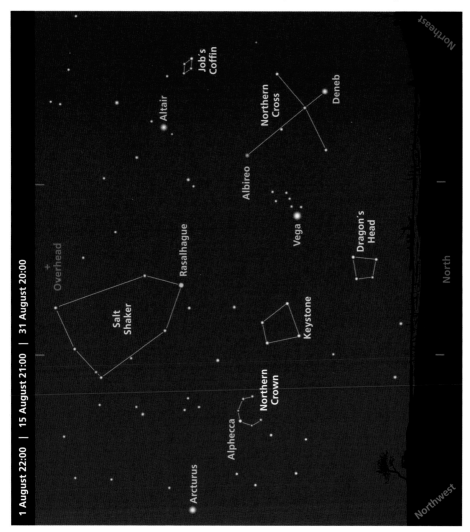

Northern stars and wonders

◆ **Vega** *(VEY-ga)*, a dazzling bluish-white star (the fifth brightest in the sky), is only about three times larger than our Sun. Early astronomers called it 'young, fresh and joyous', as opposed to golden Arcturus, which was said to be 'full of dignity'. Vega has six 'dainty' attendant stars: two making an equilateral triangle with Vega and four forming a parallelogram (seen to the upper right this month).

In Greek mythology, Vega and its attendants form the constellation Lyra the Harp, which Orpheus used to tame wild beasts. Its name, however, is derived from the Arabic for 'swooping vulture', as early Arabian starwatchers saw the star pattern as that raptor instead. Light from Vega takes only 25 years to reach Earth.

◆ **Dragon's Head** is actually the head of **Draco** *(DRAY-ko)* **the Dragon**. It is a long constellation that coils around the north celestial pole, which is about 20° (two fist-widths) below the Botswana horizon. We do not see much of this sprawling constellation, which, in some early views, represented the serpent in the Garden of Eden. What we do see prominently is its head.

In Greek mythology, Vega and its attendants form the constellation Lyra the Harp.

Vega as the eye of a steenbok

Botswana's indigenous people of the eastern Kalahari saw Vega, the brilliant star in the constellation of Lyra, as part of a male steenbok, a small African antelope.

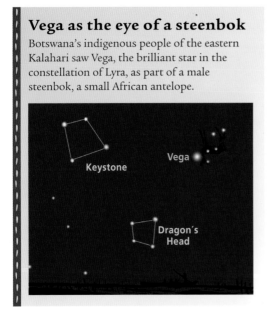

Vega derives from the Arabic word for 'swooping vulture'.

◆ **Rasalhague** *(RAHS-al-haig)* is the brightest star in the huge and dim constellation **Ophiuchus** *(Oaf-ih-YOU-kus)* **the Serpent Bearer**. It marks the position of his head. Rasalhague comes from an Arabic phrase meaning 'head of the snake charmer' (or 'serpent bearer' in this case). It is a white-hot star whose light takes only 47 years to reach our eyes. It's about 25 times brighter and four times more massive than our Sun.

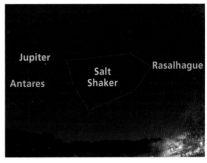

Jupiter in Ophiuchus. Compare the view with the chart below left and on page 117.

Did you know?

The thirteenth zodiac sign?
Although Ophiuchus is not a constellation of the zodiac, the Sun, Moon and planets do pass briefly through its boundaries. In the chart (below left), note how the blue line of the ecliptic (the path of the planets) passes through the white region, which outlines the boundaries of Ophiuchus. To some astrologers, this constellation represents the mysterious thirteenth sign of the zodiac. Saturn was in Ophiuchus in 2017; its position on 20 June of that year is shown as a red X in the chart. It is also labelled in the matching photograph at right taken on that date.

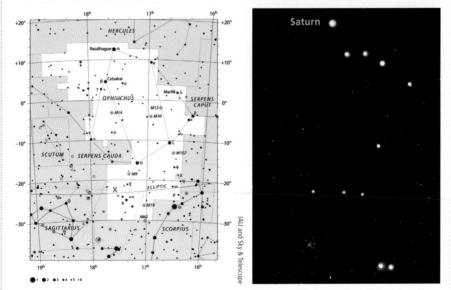

Left: Note how the blue line of the ecliptic passes through the white region outlining the boundaries of Ophiuchus. **Right:** Photo taken on 20 June 2017 showing Saturn in Opiuchus.

Did you know?

Ophiuchus

Ophiuchus is an ancient constellation representing the giant Greek healer Aesculapius *(Es-kew-LAY-Pee-us)*. We see him standing with his arms extended, gripping Serpens, a python-like constellation, which Ophiuchus holds in his hands.

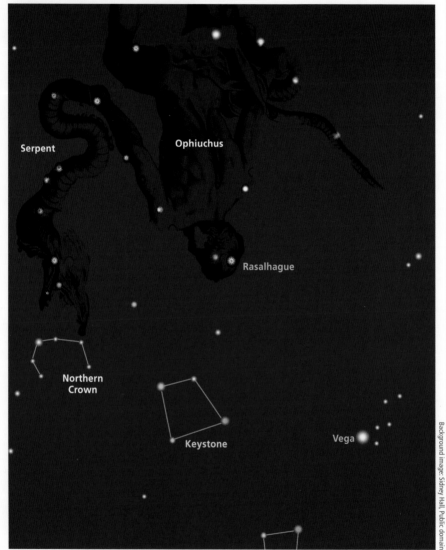

Ophiuchus is difficult to spot because the stars of this large figure form a vast hollow north of the Milky Way. Some call it the 'invisible constellation'.

The southern sky at a glance

Ara the Altar and the Southern Triangle are moving away from their highest points in the
south, leaving blue Peacock as the solitary jewel in the mid-southern sky. Above it, the
Teapot of Sagittarius lies nearly overhead, with the striking curve of the Scorpion's Tail
slightly to its southwest. Alpha and Beta Centauri point to the Southern Cross, which is
now listing towards the southwest as it heads for the horizon. Achernar shines brightly
low in the southeast, while Alnair and Fomalhaut share the mid-southeastern sky,
forming a graceful arc.

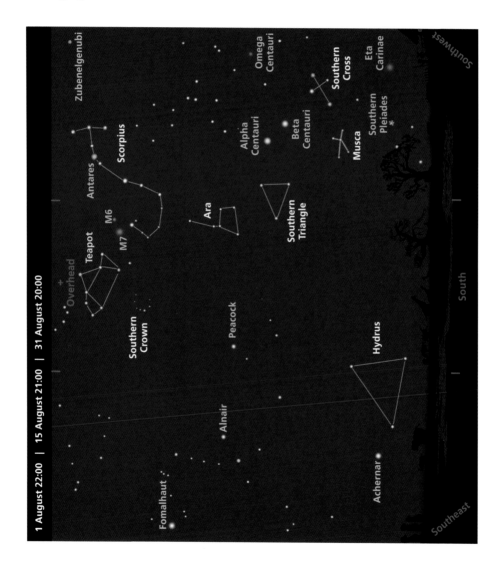

Sagittarius the Centaur.

Southern stars and wonders

◆ **The Teapot** is a star pattern within the constellation **Sagittarius** *(sa-jih-TARE-ee-us)* **the Archer**. Sagittarius is classically depicted as a Centaur (a mythological creature with the torso of a man and the lower body of a horse). We see the Centaur drawing a bow, with the arrow pointed at the Scorpion. It is in the zodiac and can be visited by the Moon and planets.

◆ **Corona Australis (the Southern Crown)** Tucked in-between two of the Centaur's hooves is the head wreath of the Centaur, which he tossed off in play. The star pattern is an attractive C-shaped laurel of about six dim, but equally bright, stars that lie close to the Centaur's belly, just south of the Teapot asterism. The wreath symbolizes a time of coming peace.

Semicircle of Corona Australis

In an old Kalahari legend, a girl who should not have been looking at a group of men sitting and eating by a rock rabbit's (dassie's) semicircular house of branches caused them to be transported to the sky as Corona Australis (the Southern Crown). We see them as they were, sitting in a semicircle around the rock rabbit's house ... perhaps they are just sitting around waiting for a spot of tea.

Corona Australis forms a wreath below the Teapot asterism.

Tempest in a teapot

The Teapot star pattern is dwarfed by the central bulge of our galaxy, within which we find the very heart of the Milky Way, near the Teapot's spout.

Galaxy Bulge

Teapot

Heart of Milky Way

Galaxy Bulge

'We' are here

NASA

Naked-eye deep sky wonders in the Sagittarius Milky Way

The abundance of stars and dust in the Milky Way near the Teapot is rich in naked-eye and binocular wonders. We've already inspected the False Comet, M6 and M7 in July. We'll now explore six more naked-eye and binocular showpieces that reveal themselves reasonably well under a dark sky.

♦ **The Great Sagittarius Star Cloud** is the most abundant region of naked-eye starlight in our Milky Way. This vast cloud of stars and dust marks the location of a spiral arm that lies between the Earth and the core of the Milky Way galaxy.

♦ **The Lagoon Nebula (M8)** is a glowing cloud of gas and starlight, visible to our unaided eyes and looking like a curdle of galactic vapour rising from the Teapot's spout. Light leaving this site of star birth takes more than 5,000 years to reach our eyes. Binoculars will show the nebula surrounding a central star cluster, which was born from this cloud of dust and gas.

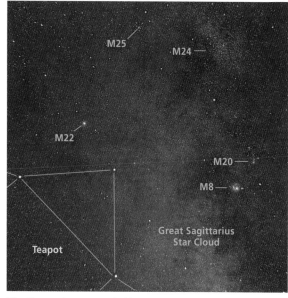

M25

M24

M22

M20

M8

Great Sagittarius
Star Cloud

Teapot

The Teapot is surrounded by an abundance of wonders.

Did you know?

Sagittarius A*

Although we cannot see it, an enormous black hole hides from view behind the dense dust and gas in the region of Sagittarius. The black hole (known as Sagittarius A* — pronounced *Sagittarius A Star*) lies at the very centre of our galaxy (marked with a red X in the photo). It is nearly 4 million times more massive than our Sun.

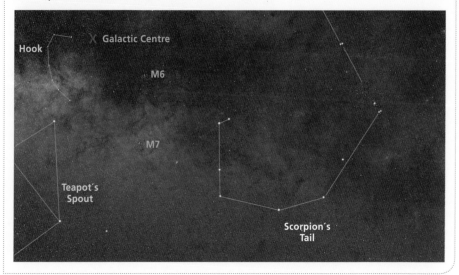

◆ **The Trifid Nebula (M20)** is another cloud of gas (both glowing and shining by reflected starlight) that appears as a little pool of mist to unaided eyes. It lies nearly at the same distance as the Lagoon Nebula. Like the Lagoon Nebula, the Trifid is a celestial crib for newly born stars.

◆ **M22** is also known as the Great Sagittarius Globular Cluster, for, as seen through a telescope, it is a globular bonfire of half a million stars blazing forth from the depths of space. To unaided eyes, it is a tight bead of light easily mistaken for a dim and diffuse star. Use averted vision to see it swell.

◆ **M24** is also known as the Small Sagittarius Star Cloud. This carpet of scintillating starlight is actually a star cloud seen through a tunnel of darkness. Countless stars are visible through this gap, created by massive veins of dust that line the spiral arm between the Earth and our galaxy's centre. We see the star cloud shining so prominently because it is framed by that dark dust. Light leaving M24 takes about 10,000 years to reach our eyes – so the light we see today left the star cloud at the end of the last Ice Age on Earth.

◆ **M25** is a young open star cluster – young for a star cluster that is, as M25 is some 95 million years old. It appears as a dim, ghostly glow to unaided eyes. Binoculars will show it as a 'tiny knot of minute glimmers', as the late-nineteenth-century astronomer Admiral Smyth described it.

The eastern sky at a glance

A string of star patterns favours the eastern sky – from the prominent Teapot of Sagittarius high overhead to the Circlet of Pisces just rising above the horizon. Between them is the large and dim Paper Boat of Capricornus (almost two fist-widths wide at its longest extent) and the tiny but conspicuous 'Y' of the Water Jar of Aquarius (which you can cover with two fingers held at arm's length). The Great Square of Pegasus is rising in the northeast, preceded by golden Enif, marking the Horse's nose. Pretty Fomalhaut rules the mid-southeastern skies, with Alnair leading it roughly at the same height above the horizon. (Turn the chart to see this correct orientation.)

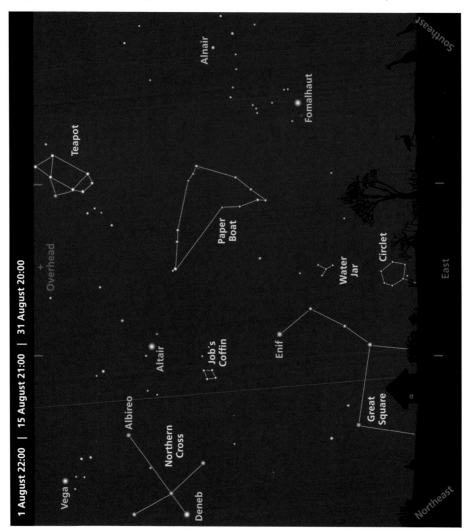

The western sky at a glance

The Scorpion and the Salt Shaker pattern of Ophiuchus dominate the high western sky. Libra's Balance Stars, Zubeneschamali and Zubenelgenubi, commandeer the mid-western sky. Spica in Virgo and the Sail of Corvus are ready for setting in the west. Alpha and Beta Centauri are still glistening in the southwestern sky, though the Southern Cross is slipping towards the horizon. Golden Arcturus is the most prominent star in the northwestern sky, flanked by the delicate Northern Crown.

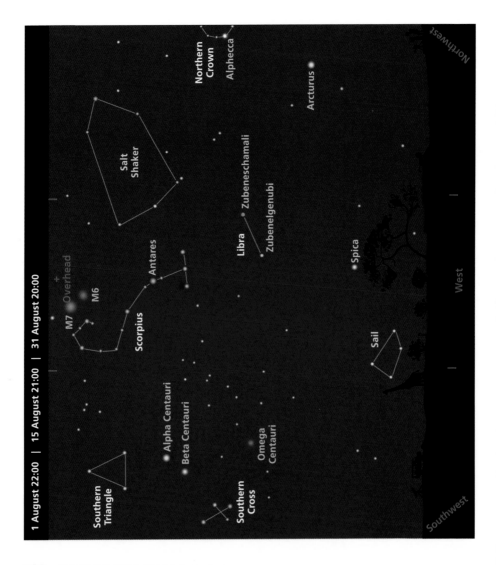

1 August 22:00 | 15 August 21:00 | 31 August 20:00

The northern sky at a glance

Deneb has reached its highest position above the northern horizon as seen from Botswana. Two star patterns are also at or near their best: the Northern Cross (with Deneb marking its top) and the diamond of Delphinus, otherwise known as Job's Coffin. Altair has passed its highest point and is joining Vega on a march towards the northwestern sky, where the Dragon's Head nears setting. Enif is advancing into the realm of the north followed by three star patterns: the 'Y' of the Water Jar of Aquarius, the Circlet of Pisces and the Great Square of Pegasus.

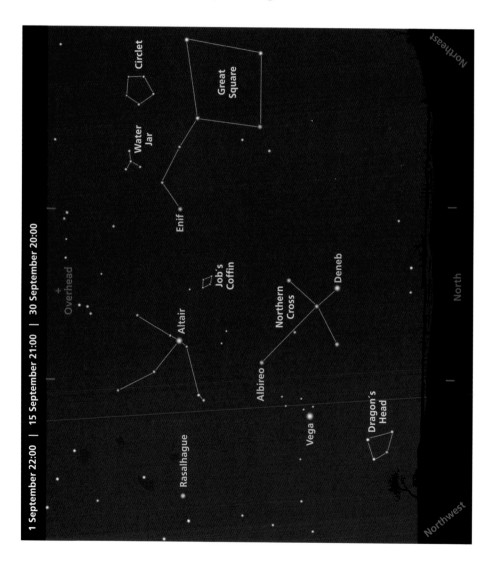

Northern stars and wonders

◆ **Deneb** *(DEN-ebb)* is a scintillating gem that lies in one of the densest regions of the northern Milky Way. It marks the top of the Northern Cross – a familiar star pattern. The Northern Cross is much larger than the Southern Cross. You can cover the Southern Cross with a fist held at arm's length, but the Northern Cross is double the length. Deneb is the brightest star in the constellation of **Cygnus** *(SIG-nus)* the Swan,

Cygnus the African Jacana

The Cygnus constellation appears to fly over the river of the Milky Way, just as a yellow-billed stork flies over the Okavango River. In classical mythology, Cygnus is the great god Zeus disguised as a swan to win the love of Leda, who adored swans. While swans do not grace the Botswana landscape, it takes little imagination to transform Cygnus the Swan into a yellow-billed stork or an African Jacana in flight. The African Jacana is sometimes referred to as the Jesus bird, which seems appropriate as the brightest stars in Cygnus also form the Northern Cross – a star pattern representing Christ's crucifixion; although the real reason the Jacana is called the Jesus bird is because it appears to walk on water as it moves from lily pad to lily pad.

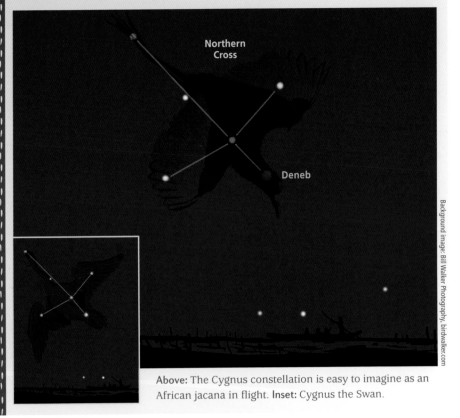

Northern Cross

Deneb

Background image: Bill Walker Photography, birdwalker.com

Above: The Cygnus constellation is easy to imagine as an African jacana in flight. **Inset:** Cygnus the Swan.

and marks the bird's tail. Deneb is a distant supergiant star that is 100 times larger than our Sun and shines more than 50,000 times more brightly. Although nearby Vega outshines Deneb, Deneb is about 1,000 times more distant. If we could reel in Deneb to the distance of Vega, Deneb would greatly outshine it – and the planet Venus too! It takes light leaving Deneb 1,500 years to reach our eyes.

◆ **Albireo** *(al-BEE-ri-oh)* is an orange giant star marking the beak of Cygnus the Swan. Early Arab skywatchers saw it as the beak of a hen. Although distant, Albireo shines so brightly because it is about 100 times larger and 1,000 times brighter than our Sun. The second brightest star in the constellation, Albireo's light takes 380 years to reach our eyes. A strong pair of binoculars held very still can split the star into two components – one gold, the other blue or green – the colours seen depend on the observer's eyesight.

◆ **Altair** *(AL-tair)* is the brightest star in **Aquila** *(ack-WILL-lah)* the Eagle, though Arabian stargazers saw it as a vulture. A white-hot star, Altair shines 10 times brighter than our Sun. It appears so prominent because it is very close. Its light takes only 17 years to reach our eyes. Two fainter golden stars attend to Altair, and together they are known as the Family of Aquila. Three fingers held at arm's length will cover the Family. In classical mythology, Aquila is the bird that carried the thunderbolts of Zeus.

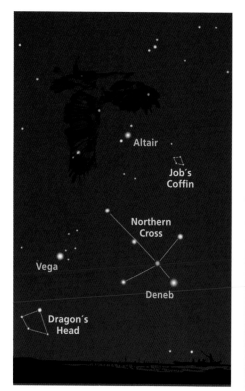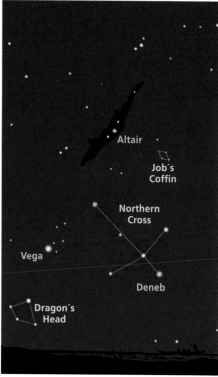

From Botswana, we can imagine a fish eagle in the stars of Aquila (left), as well as a crocodile (right). Astrologically, Altair warned of danger from reptiles (like crocodiles).

◆ **Job's Coffin** is an alluring diamond-shaped star pattern in **Delphinus** *(DELL-fee-nus)* the Dolphin. In ancient Egypt, the dolphin was a symbol of resurrection. Biblically interpreted, the Coffin is the confining hedge that God placed around Job. It may also be a misnomer for Jonah's Coffin, as in the biblical Jonah, who was swallowed by a whale and entombed.

In classical mythology, the dolphin served as a messenger of the sea-god, Poseidon. In the night sky, the body of the Dolphin is the diamond-shaped star pattern, while the tail is a fainter star nearby.

Did you know?

Aquila in the Crucifixion scene
Early Christians saw Altair as the head of Christ, and its two reddish companions as a crown of thorns. The outstretched wings of the Eagle became the outstretched arms of Christ on the Crucifix.

Job's Coffin is an ancient sign of resurrection. The Coffin could also symbolize the slab of stone that sealed Jesus in his tomb before the resurrection.

Diego Velázquez Wikimedia Commons, Public domain

Altair

The Crucifixion

Job's Coffin

Altair is the brightest star in the centre of the Crucifixion scene, with the slab of Job's Coffin alongside.

The ant larvae of Altair

Lucy Catherine Lloyd (1834–1914), together with Wilhelm Bleek (1827–1875), created a nineteenth-century archive of |Xam and !Kung texts. Her journal entry dated 13 October 1873 associates the coming of Altair in the sky with the season for harvesting ant larvae for food. According to her entry, when Altair 'comes out', ant larvae fatten and become white, as seen in the extract below.

This time corresponds with the season of Botswana's first rains; when the ant larvae detect that the ground is wet, they move closer to the surface, where they can be harvested near holes in the ground. The tale thus associates Altair with the coming of the first rains.

The indigenous people of western Botswana imagined Altair and its attendant stars as a female steenbok. In August, Vega was imagined as a male steenbok.

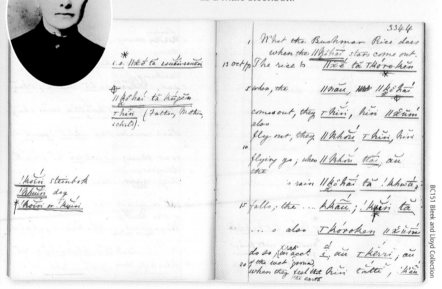

Lucy Catherine Lloyd documented |Xam and !Kung texts; an extract from Lloyd's journal details the appearance of Altair ('Father, Mother and Child stars') and ant larvae ('rice').

The southern sky at a glance

Three blue stars adorn the south and southeastern skies, with pretty Peacock leading the way, and Alnair and Achernar following. The Teapot of Sagittarius dominates the view high in the southwestern sky, now that red Antares and the striking curve of the Scorpion's tail have moved into the mid-southwestern sky. The Milky Way pours from the spout of the Teapot, through the stars of the Scorpion and beyond. The Small Magellanic Cloud is on the rise and may be too low to be seen well, it is so diffuse. We are losing the Southern Cross, which is now very low to the southwest horizon. Alpha and Beta Centauri will also soon be ready to slip off the celestial stage, followed by the Southern Triangle.

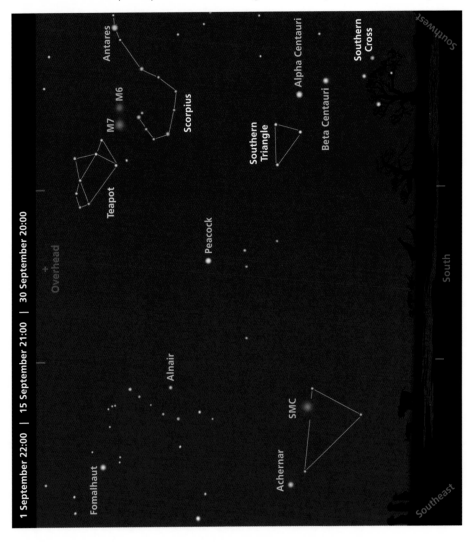

The eastern sky at a glance

Lonely Fomalhaut rules the mid-eastern sky, which is largely devoid of bright starlight or the Milky Way. Capricorn's Paper Boat star pattern is sailing high above Fomalhaut. Three blue gems – Achernar, Peacock and Alnair – roam the southeastern sky. Three asterisms (one great and two small) have risen to a respectable height in the northeast: the Great Square of Pegasus (each side as wide as your fist held at arm's length), the Y-shaped Water Jar of Aquarius (which can be covered with two fingers), and the slightly larger Circlet of Pisces. The Andromeda Galaxy has also risen in the northeast; its misty glow may be better seen when higher in the sky. Deneb Kaitos twinkles about two fists above the east-southeast horizon.

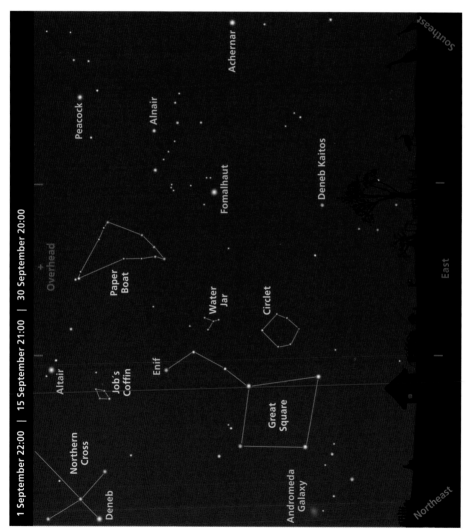

1 September 22:00 | 15 September 21:00 | 30 September 20:00

Eastern stars and wonders

This month the eastern sky is a water world filled with classical images of water signs: **Capricornus** *(CAP-rih- CORN-us)* the Sea Goat; the **Water Jar of Aquarius** *(uh-KWAIR-ee-us)*; one of the two fishes of **Pisces** *(PIE-sees)*; **Cetus** *(SEE-tus)* the Sea Monster, which is rising tail first; and **Piscis Austrinis** *(PIE-sis oss-TREE-nus)* the Southern Fish. Three of these constellations, Capricornus, Aquarius and Pisces, are in the path of the planets, so the Moon and planets occasionally visit these regions, confusing the view.

This watery theme originated with the Sun's passage through this region of sky during the rainy season of ancient Middle Eastern lands. Specifically, it ties in with the great flood in the Tigris–Euphrates basin of ancient Mesopotamia, which some researchers have linked to the Great Flood in Genesis.

For the ancients, the sea was deep and dark, and inscrutable. For them, the dim stars in this region of the night sky most likely mirrored the unfathomable depths of the sea, so the creators of the constellations populated them with creatures they could only imagine must live in its mysterious waters.

Below: A Blood Moon (total lunar eclipse) and the planet Mars in Capricornus, as they appeared on 27 July 2018.
Right: The red planet Mars on the cusp of Aquarius and Pisces.

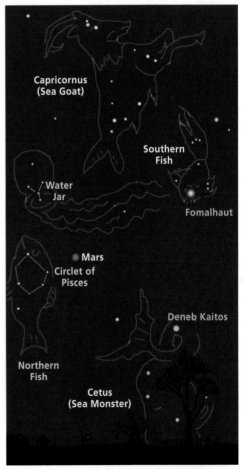

The western sky at a glance

The Teapot of Sagittarius and the Scorpion are tumbling down towards the horizon, with the Milky Way running through them. The Balance Stars of Libra (Zubeneschamali and Zubenelgenubi) are ready to set in the west. The two celestial crowns (Northern and Southern) lie on opposite sides of the sky: the Southern Crown high in the south-southwest and the Northern Crown (together with the Keystone of Hercules) low in the northwest, near setting. (Turn the chart to see the correct orientation.)

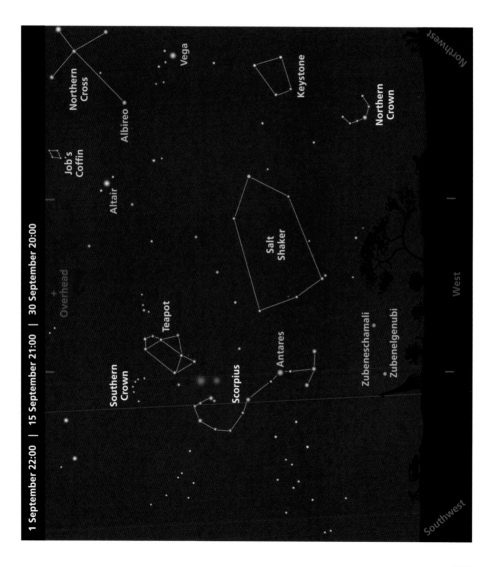

The northern sky at a glance

Enif, the nose of the celestial horse, has galloped to its highest point in the north. We see it joined by the Great Square of Pegasus, the 'Y' of the Water Jar (of Aquarius) and the Circlet of Pisces. Very low in the north, the 'M' star pattern of Cassiopeia is rising from its earthen tomb. Between it and the Great Square is the dim and delicate glow of the Andromeda Galaxy. Deneb in the Northern Cross and the diamond of Job's Coffin are following Altair and Vega towards the northwest, while three golden stars (Mirach, Almach and Hamal) are better placed for viewing in the northeast.

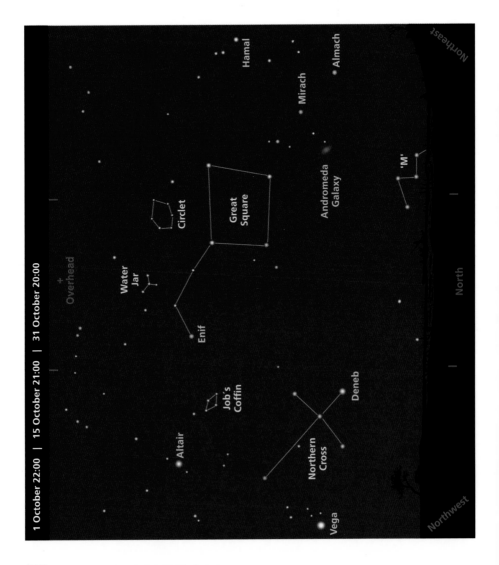

Northern stars and wonders

◆ **Enif** *(EEN-if)* is the brightest star in **Pegasus** *(PEG-uh-suss)*, the Winged Horse of classical mythology. Pegasus was born from the blood that dripped from the serpent-haired Medusa's head, into the ocean. The Greeks imagined the horse in the process of leaping out from that bloody sea foam, so we do not see its full body, only half of it. The word Pegasus is derived from a Greek word meaning to 'spring forth' – and so they named the constellations after creatures they could only have imagined lived in the mysterious depths of the Earth's oceans.

Enif shines with a noticeable golden hue and marks the Horse's nose. Its Arabic name refers to the Horse's nose, lips, jaws or muzzle. An orange supergiant, Enif is 300 times larger and 6,700 times more luminous than our Sun. If we could replace our Sun with Enif, the star would fill nearly half our sky. Enif is likely destined to become a supernova, meaning it will end its life with a catastrophic explosion. If it exploded today, we wouldn't know about it for 670 years, as that's how long it takes for the star's light to reach our eyes.

◆ **The Great Square of Pegasus** marks the body of the winged horse. It may be a challenge to pick it out among the stars because its four bright stars are widely set about by nearly 15° of sky. Your fist held at arm's length will comfortably fit within the Great Square, so use that as a guide.

Pegasus swoops through the Great Square.

Background image: Sidney Hall, Public domain

Kingfisher and bream

We have already encountered the Water Jar and Circlet of Pisces star patterns in September, seeing how they belong to an ancient celestial water world imagined by early stargazers. In keeping with that theme, but bringing it into the twenty-first century, we can also imagine the Water Jar as a pied kingfisher hovering above a river, while the stars in the Circlet of Pisces make a good-looking bream.

The southern sky at a glance

The Paper Boat of Capricornus has moved into the high southern sky, pushing the Teapot of Sagittarius off its lofty perch. The Teapot is now falling towards the west-southwest, spilling its milky vapours towards the horizon. Pretty Peacock has left centre stage, allowing Alnair in Grus the Crane to take its place. Swimming above the Crane is lonely and bright Fomalhaut in the Southern Fish. Alpha and Beta Centauri, along with the Southern Triangle, lie low in the southwest, while Achernar and the Small Magellanic Cloud are moving ever closer to their highest point above the southern horizon.

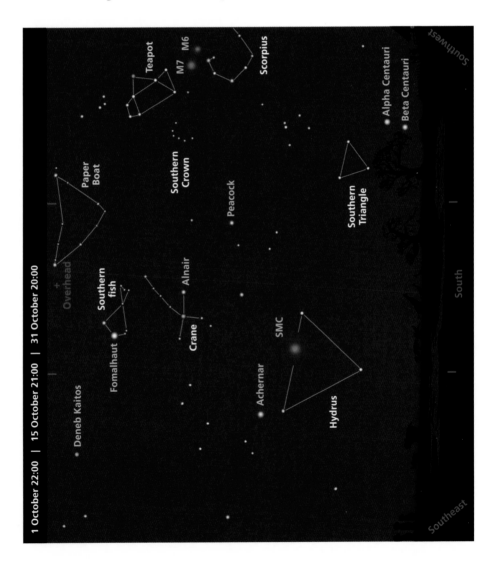

Southern stars and wonders

◆ **Peacock** is the brightest star in the constellation **Pavo** *(PAH-vo)* **the Peacock**. This more recently named star was once used by pilots to navigate their planes in the days prior to GPS. Peacock shines as brightly as a star in Orion's Belt and is a hot-blue luminary, eight times larger than our Sun. Light leaving the star takes 180 years to reach our eyes.

◆ **Alnair** *(AL-near)* is the brightest star in **Grus** *(GROOS)* **the Crane**. Alnair's name is Arabic for 'the bright one'. It is a hot-blue subgiant, about three times larger than our Sun. Like all hot stars, it spins remarkably fast – some 230 kilometres per second, or 120 times faster than our Sun. Light leaving its surface takes about 100 years to reach our eyes.

◆ **Fomalhaut** *(FO-mal-ought)* is the alpha star in **Piscis Austrinus** *(PIE-sis oss-TREE-nus)*, which means the Southern Fish. (The Northern Fishes are known as Pisces.) Fomalhaut is a white-hot star – 16 times more luminous than, and twice the size of, our Sun. Light leaving its surface takes about 25 years to reach our eyes. Although we cannot see it, the star is surrounded by a disc of debris that may, one day, form into a solar system like our own.

Botswana's celestial wilderness

Imagine Botswana's skies as a celestial wilderness to explore on a night-time safari.

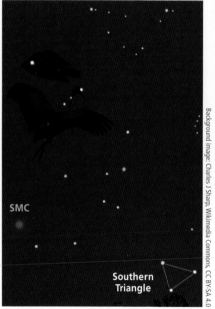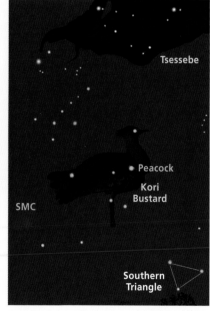

Background image: Charles J Sharp, Wikimedia Commons, CC BY-SA 4.0

Left: Piscis Austrinus, the Southern Fish can be imagined as a bream in the waters of the high southern skies, over which a wattled crane flies. **Right:** The Paper Boat of Capricornus (at the very top of the image) transforms into a tsessebe, although a hartebeest would work just as well. The stars of Pavo the Peacock can also form the kori bustard – the world's heaviest flying bird and Botswana's national bird.

The eastern sky at a glance

Fomalhaut has slipped off centre stage, making way for two orange stars, Deneb Kaitos and Menkar, both in Cetus. This part of the sky remains devoid of bright starlight or light from the Milky Way (unless the variable Mira blazes into view; see December for details). The blue gems, Achernar and Peacock, dominate the southeastern and southern sky. The Great Square of Pegasus, the Y-shaped Water Jar of Aquarius and the slightly larger Circlet of Pisces have moved higher into the northeastern sky, as has the Andromeda Galaxy. (Rotate the chart to see the correct orientation.) Lower in the northeast lies the golden gem, Hamal, in Aries the Ram. It marks the location of the zodiac; the Moon and planets can pass by.

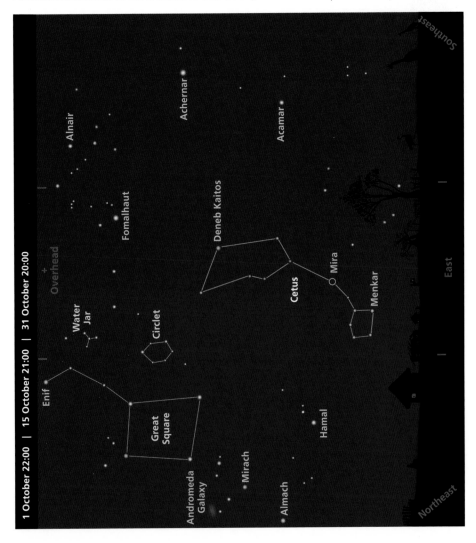

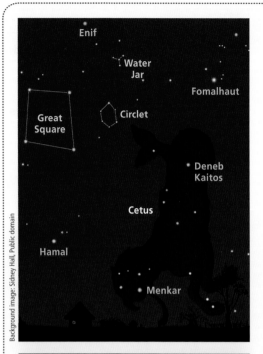

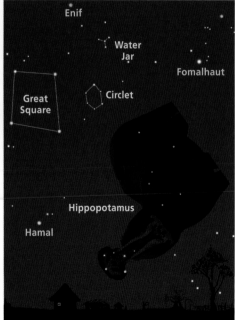

Background image: Sidney Hall, Public domain

Monster tales

Cetus the Sea Monster

Cetus is the fourth largest constellation in the sky. Ancient stargazers imagined it as a hideous beast from the sea. This aquatic Frankenstein's monster has the head and neck of either a lion or a dragon, the torso of a horse and the coiling tail of a sea serpent. In classical mythology, Cetus is the monster that the sea nymphs sent to devour the Chained Maiden, Andromeda. It is also popularly known as Cetus the Whale.

Cetus's two brightest stars, Deneb Kaitos and Menkar, are highest in the north in November and December, respectively. Turn to pages 126 and 135 for more information.

Cetus as hippopotamus

Using your imagination, the stars of Cetus can be seen as another 'whale of a monster': a hippopotamus, the most dangerous mammal in Africa and the world's third largest mammal. The hippo makes an appropriate substitute for Cetus, as its closest relative is the whale. Furthermore, the name hippopotamus is Greek for 'river horse', which reinforces its association with the aquatic Cetus.

Top: An interpretation of Cetus is shown centre stage in October. Use your imagination to perceive the stars of Cetus as a frightening beast. **Bottom:** Cetus is depicted as a hippopotamus or 'river horse'.

October

The western sky at a glance

The Scorpion is falling head first into the south-southwestern horizon, and will be followed shortly by the Teapot of Sagittarius and the hub of the Milky Way. In the northwest, Rasalhague is neck and neck with Antares in that race. The Paper Boat of Capricornus is beautifully positioned for viewing in the high western sky. Altair and Job's Coffin lie to its northwest, where Vega continues to dip lower in the sky, followed farther north by Deneb. Now is a good time to compare the Northern Cross star pattern with the other crucifix represented by Altair and neighbouring stars (described on page 112).

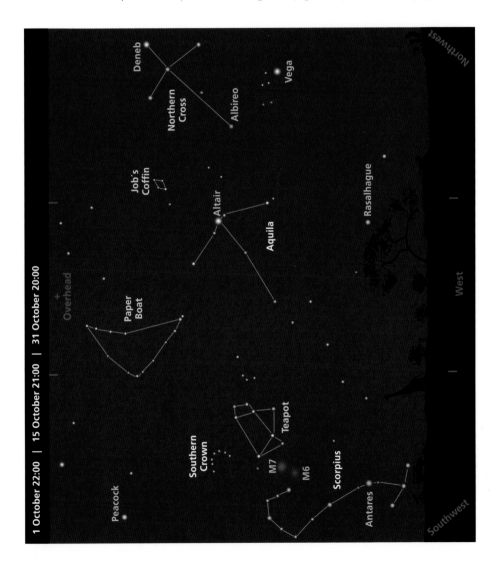

124 MONTHLY STAR CHARTS October

The northern sky at a glance

The Great Square of Pegasus is heading towards the northwest, with the Water Jar of Aquarius and the Circlet of Pisces keeping pace. Deneb is preparing an exit low in the northwest. Deneb Kaitos, the tail of Cetus the Sea Monster, has claimed the northern sky overhead. The 'M' pattern of Cassiopeia is nearing its highest position, though it will remain low to the northern horizon. Above it is the dim ellipse of the Andromeda Galaxy flanked by golden Mirach. Hamal makes a gentle arc with Algol and Mirfak, which arches over the Northern Triangle and golden Almach. In the east, Menkar and the variable star, Mira (if it is visible), arc midway up the sky with the Pleiades.

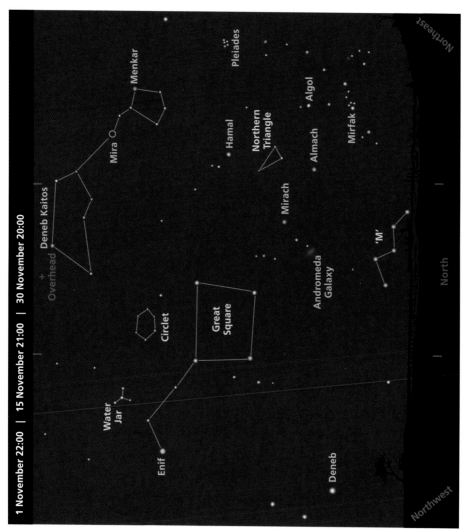

1 November 22:00 | 15 November 21:00 | 30 November 20:00

Northern stars and wonders

◆ **Deneb Kaitos** *(DEN-ebb KAI-tos)* Even though the ancients labelled Deneb Kaitos as the constellation's Beta star, it shines as its brightest. Deneb Kaitos is an Arabic word meaning 'whale's tail', and refers to its position in the constellation of Cetus the Sea Monster (as described in October's eastern sky). The two eastern stars in the Great Square almost point to it. Follow an imaginary line upwards from the two eastern stars, about twice the distance of the eastern side of the Great Square; Deneb Kaitos will be the brightest star in the region. It is an orange giant about 35 times larger and 145 times more luminous than our Sun. It is also relatively nearby; light leaving its surface takes only 96 years to reach our eyes.

◆ **Mirach** *(MIRR-ack)* is the Beta star of Andromeda, the Chained Maiden. The word 'Mirach' is derived from an Arabic phrase suggesting a girdle or waist cloth, as the star marks the maiden's left hip. Mirach is a red giant star, three times more massive and nearly 2,000 times more luminous than our Sun. If we could replace our Sun with Mirach, its belly would extend all the way out to the orbit of Mercury, the planet closest to the Sun. Light leaving its surface takes about 200 years to reach our eyes.

◆ **The Andromeda Galaxy** *(an-DRAH-mih-duh)* is part of the dim fabric of the naked-eye sky. Mirach will lead the way to it. Mirach is the brightest star in a north-northwest trending chain of three stars. The Andromeda Galaxy is just below and a little west of the third (and faintest) star. Under a dark sky, those with keen eyesight can see this phantom ellipse of light without optical aid. If you spy it, you will be looking through

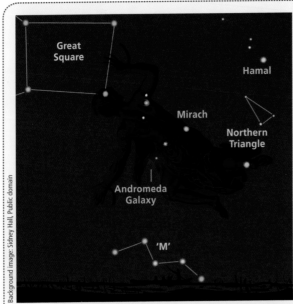

Andromeda the Chained Maiden is seen as a curved line of four bright stars suspended over Cassiopeia.

Andromeda the Chained Maiden

The name Andromeda translates into 'she who reigns over humanity'. Andromeda is the daughter of Cepheus and Cassiopeia (the 'M' star pattern in the charts shown here), the mythical King and Queen of Ethiopia. Cepheus offered Andromeda as a sacrifice to Cetus the Sea Monster – to appease the sea nymphs after his wife had angered them with her vanity. We see Andromeda in the sky as a beautiful princess (left), head resting on Pegasus, the forest of stars in our galaxy, then across a great gulf of empty space, at another island universe similar to that of our own Milky Way Galaxy. Light takes about 2.5 million years to reach our eyes from this distant neighbour, so we see the galaxy as it was 2.5 million years in the past. Astronomers now believe that, in about 4.5 billion years, the Andromeda Galaxy will collide with the Milky Way and the two will become one.

Follow the trail of three stars from Mirach to the Andromeda Galaxy. Although it can be seen with unaided eyes, it is better observed through binoculars, appearing like a phantom ellipse of light with a bright central core. Orange Mirach can be seen at top right with binoculars.

arms open and chained to a rock. Perseus the Hero swooped down to save Andromeda from the gaping jaws of Cetus, and bore her away in triumph.

The main star pattern of Andromeda is a slightly curved line of four bright stars. When this row is combined with the Great Square of Pegasus, the star pattern looks like an immense, upside-down saucepan (right).

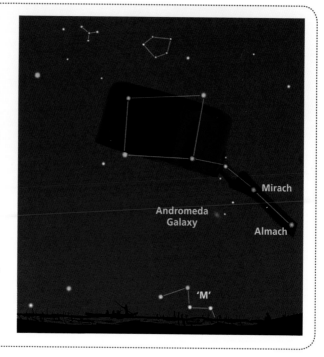

The Great Square of Pegasus and the brightest stars in Andromeda can be imagined as a saucepan.

Wildlife in the night skies

Andromeda as a Lion

As the indigenous people of Botswana generally associated reddish stars with predators, we can imagine the chain of orange stars in Andromeda to represent a lion. Mirach would be near the animal's heart.

One could also picture the three stars in the chain as three lions, or leopards or cheetahs.

From the Botswana wilderness, it is fitting to see the stars of Pegasus as the familiar striped African equid – a zebra – as it migrates across the sky.

Cassiopeia as African Skimmers

The 'M' star pattern of Cassiopeia is classically rendered as Queen Cassiopeia's throne, on which she is seated. But we do not see the Queen in her entirety from Botswana. As only its M-shaped star pattern 'skims' Botswana's northern horizon, it is more appropriately seen as a flock of African skimmers. These near-threatened birds fly in lines just above water level and use their lower mandible to scoop up small fish on which they feed.

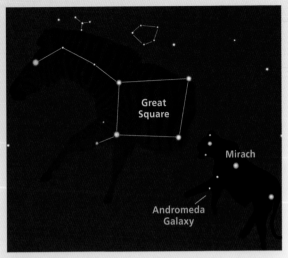

Andromeda's orange stars can be imagined as a lion following in the footsteps of Pegasus or a zebra.

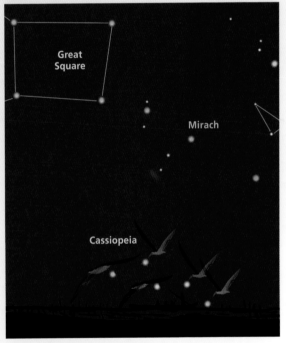

The 'M' star pattern of Cassiopeia looks like a flock of African skimmers just above the horizon.

The southern sky at a glance

Alnair and Fomalhaut have left centre stage. Hydrus the Male Water Snake and the Small Magellanic Cloud are now at their prime viewing location. Achernar, at the end of the celestial river (Eridanus), is marching towards its highest position in the south, followed by its fellow river star Acamar. The Large Magellanic Cloud and Canopus return to the celestial stage in the southeast as we near the year's end. In the southwest, the Southern Triangle is preparing to slip below the horizon. The Southern Crown is also nearing setting towards the southwest. The bluish wonder Peacock is the most prominent star in the mid-southwestern sky; it too is heading towards setting in the southwest.

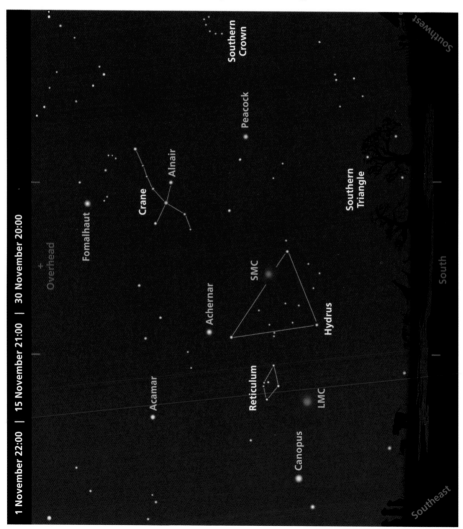

1 November 22:00 | 15 November 21:00 | 30 November 20:00

Southern stars and wonders

◆ **The Small Magellanic Cloud (SMC)** is a dwarf satellite galaxy orbiting our Milky Way. Like the Large Magellanic Cloud (LMC, described in January), it is named in honour of the Portuguese navigator, Ferdinand Magellan, who described both clouds in 1519 (although indigenous people would have observed them much earlier). Like the LMC, the SMC is not a cloud at all, but a mini-galaxy 210,000 light years beyond our Milky Way (or 30 light years more distant than the LMC). Binoculars show some of the SMC's individual stars, nebulae and star clusters. Binoculars will also show two globular star clusters: tiny NGC 362 and magnificent 47 Tucanae.

◆ **47 Tucanae** *(too-KAH-nee)* Under a dark sky, the dim, fuzzy glow of 47 Tucanae is just visible to the unaided eye near the SMC. The cluster may contain half a million stars!

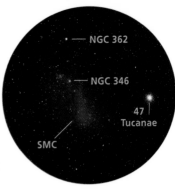

Binoculars will reveal the wonders of the Small Magellanic Cloud in November. The pear-shaped galaxy appears warped, with a bright star-forming region (NGC 346) near its tip.

Hubble Space Telescope

European Southern Observatory

Above: The star-forming region NGC 346 in the Small Magellanic Cloud. **Inset:** This Hubble Space Telescope image shows the core of the globular star cluster, 47 Tucanae, which lies some 15,000 light years distant.

The eastern sky at a glance

Orion is rising above the eastern horizon with brilliant Rigel in the lead. From Rigel flows the long and meandering constellation of Eridanus the River, identified by its bright stars Acamar and Achernar (marking the end). Deneb Kaitos (the tail of Cetus the Sea Monster) shines high overhead. Variable star Mira (if it is visible in the neck of Cetus), together with Menkar, points towards orange Aldebaran, now low in the northeast. Golden Hamal rules the mid-northeastern sky, while the fuzzy starlight of the Pleiades lies almost between it and Aldebaran. Be sure to turn the star chart to see the proper orientation.

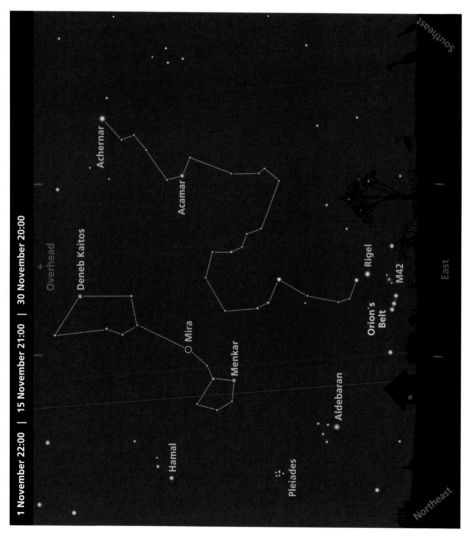

Did you know?

Eridanus the River

Eridanus the River is the sixth largest constellation in the sky. All constellations are measured by the area covered within their official boundaries, not their length. While Eridanus is long and meandering, it is also a thin constellation.

Different cultures have associated the celestial river with the great rivers in their own lands. In ancient Egypt, it represented the Nile; in Persia, the Tigris or Euphrates; and in Greece, the River of the Ocean. In Botswana, it has been interpreted as the country's most important wetland feature, the Okavango River.

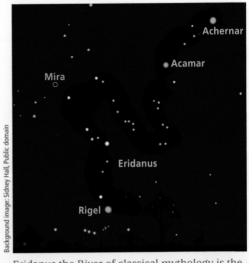

Background image: Sidney Hall, Public domain

Eridanus the River of classical mythology is the sixth largest constellation in the sky.

The photo of the meandering Okavango River superimposed on the celestial river shows how Eridanus can easily be imagined to resemble the Okavango.

The western sky at a glance

The mid-western sky is devoid of bright stars, except for Enif, the nose of Pegasus the Winged Horse, which dominates the mid-west-northwestern sky, while Fomalhaut burns high just south of west. The Paper Boat of Capricornus is sinking closer to the horizon, while Altair in the celestial Eagle is preparing to set in the early hours of the night. The Teapot of Sagittarius has emptied its galactic vapours into the southwestern horizon, where the Southern Crown will soon head. Deneb and the Northern Cross are ready to set in the northwestern sky, and will soon be followed by Job's Coffin.

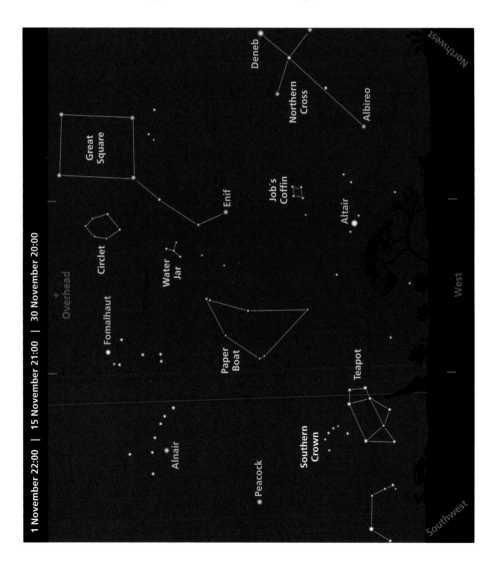

The northern sky at a glance

The northern sky is scattered with soft starlight. Nothing bold and outstanding graces the celestial landscape – unless a bright planet is drifting through the zodiac (near the Circlet of Pisces, Hamal in Aries or the Pleiades). Without any planets in view, Hamal in Aries the Ram is like the north central spotlight, with Almach in Andromeda directly below it. In-between these two colourful stars is the delicate form of the Northern Triangle. Menkar is also near centre stage – though it could be outshone by Mira the Wonderful, if it has risen to maximum brightness. The 'M' of Cassiopeia is still holding its own, but it will start to slip below the horizon as the night progresses. The Great

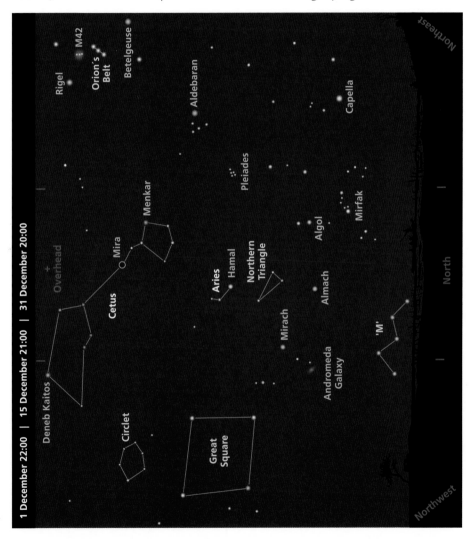

1 December 22:00 | 15 December 21:00 | 31 December 20:00

Square of Pegasus and the Circlet of Pisces have moved into the northwestern sky, while, in the northeast, we see the return of Mirfak (described in January), Capella, Aldebaran and the stars of Orion, which are described in February (see pp. 42–44).

Northern stars and wonders

◆ **Menkar** *(men-KAHR)* Although Menkar is labelled the Alpha star of Cetus the Sea Monster (see October), it is only the second brightest; the brightest star in the constellation is its Beta star, Deneb Kaitos, in the Sea Monster's tail (see November). It is possible that Menkar may have faded over the course of thousands of years. The star's name is Arabic for 'the Nose', and it refers to the star's position on the head of the classical Sea Monster. Menkar is a red giant star, 170 times larger and 380 times more luminous than our Sun. Light leaving its surface takes about 220 years to reach our eyes.

◆ **Hamal** *(HAM-al)* is the brightest star in the zodiacal constellation **Aries** *(AIR-ease)* the Ram. The name Aries is derived from an Arabic word meaning 'the Ram'; the star itself represents the entire constellation. Over 2,000 years ago, the Sun was near Hamal the Ram during the time of the spring equinox in the northern hemisphere. The star is a sizable orange giant, being some 15 times larger and 90 times brighter than our Sun. Light leaving its surface takes only 66 years to reach our eyes.

Aries as Hyena

The constellation of Aries is most commonly recognized by Hamal and an arc of two or three stars nearby (depending on how clear the sky is).

Aries can be imagined as a hyena, as the golden-orange colour of Hamal was often associated with predators or carnivores in local sky lore.

Hamal gives Aries a warm glow.

If we could see Mira with ultraviolet eyes, we'd see that it deposits material in its wake as it moves forward.

◆ **Mira** *(MY-rah)* Mira the Wonderful is one of the night sky's most amazing naked-eye stars. It is a variable star, so it changes brightness. Usually the star is not visible to the unaided eye, but about every 330 days (roughly only once a year), it comes into naked-eye view, burning with a Mars-like redness. Mira is a whopping red giant star some 1,000 times larger and 8,500 times more luminous than our Sun. Mira is whipping through space at 130 kilometres per second. If we could replace our Sun with Mira, its belly would extend so far that our Earth would be inside the star's cool atmosphere. The star is somewhat distended because it is nearing the end of its life. Mira's appearance is prescient of our Sun's appearance in another 5 billion years. Light leaving this star takes about 420 years to reach our eyes.

◆ **Almach** *(ALL-mach)* is a word derived from an early Arabic phrase meaning 'predatory animal' – perhaps a honey badger, or wild dog or cat. Try to envision one of these animals as a star when you see them in the wild. Today the star marks one of Andromeda's feet. Although we cannot see it, Almach is a dynamic triple star. Its brightest member (the one we see) is an orange giant star, 160 times larger and 2,000 times brighter than our Sun. It looks so dim because it is far away, taking light some 355 years to reach our eyes.

Almach is shown here as the bright eye of a wild dog (or painted wolf).

NASA/JPL-Caltech

Mira the Wonderful

Mira is an amazing star – only visible sometimes. This red giant star is in its final death throes and is undergoing vast pulsations.

In some classical legends, Mira, a burning lump of coal, was thrust into the throat of Cetus the Sea Monster, to kill it. This drama repeats itself about once a year. Once the star achieves maximum brightness, it can remain visible for about 10 days before it starts to fade. Mira achieved maximum brightness around 20 December 2019. As maximum brightness occurs about once every 11 months, we can expect it to be bright again sometime around 20 November 2020, 20 October 2021 and so on. The star can behave erratically, so it may not always appear when predicted.

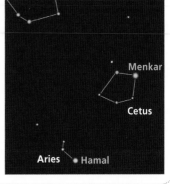

Top right: When Mira is visible, it 'completes' the constellation, as it fills the gap between the pentagram of Cetus the Monster's oval head and the stars that form its body. **Right:** When Mira is not visible, Cetus's head appears severed from the rest of its body and the constellation appears as two independent groups of stars.

The southern sky at a glance

Acamar and Archernar, the two drainage points of the celestial river, Eridanus, split centre stage with the Large and Small Magellanic Clouds (LMC and SMC). The Triangle of Hydrus is also prominent, with little Reticulum (described in January) almost lost among them. Peacock, Alnair and Fomalhaut have lined up almost parallel to the west-southwest horizon. Canopus, the False Cross and the Diamond Cross are once again moving into the southeastern sky, in preparation for the new year to begin.

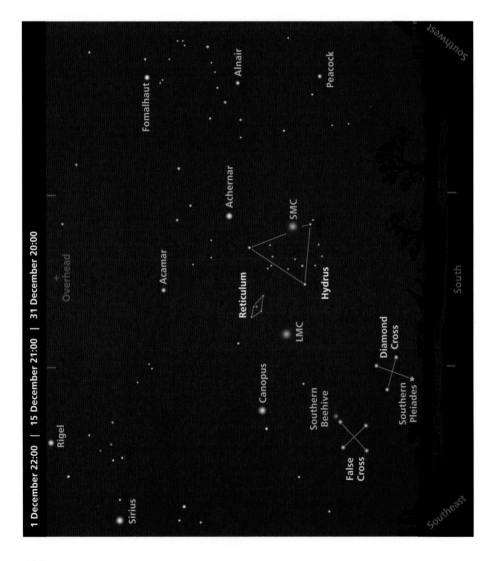

◆ **Achernar** *(AK-er-nar)*, meaning 'the end of the river' in Arabic, marks the terminus of Eridanus the River. Achernar is a hot-blue star about 15 times larger and 2,700 times more luminous than the Sun. Light leaving its surface takes 140 years to reach our eyes. If we could see the star as well as we see our Sun, it would appear highly flattened, due to its rapid rotation. This massive star spins on its axis once every two days, as opposed to our Sun, which takes about a month to spin on its axis.

◆ **Acamar** *(AH-kuh-mar)* also derives from an Arabic phrase meaning 'the end of the river'. At one time, the celestial river did indeed end at Acamar – at least as seen from Greece. European navigators extended the river once they saw the more magnificent Achernar (a little bit farther to the south) connected to Acamar by a stream of five stars. Acamar is a blue giant star, nearly 100 times more luminous than our Sun. Light leaving the surface of this star takes 160 years to reach our eyes.

Eridanus as Ostrich

Eridanus the River has been compared with the Okavango River. In Arabia, early stargazers saw a group of ostriches among its stars, both young and old, as well as some ostrich nests, eggs and eggshells.

Ancient tribes in North Africa also depicted the stars of Eridanus as a group of ostriches.

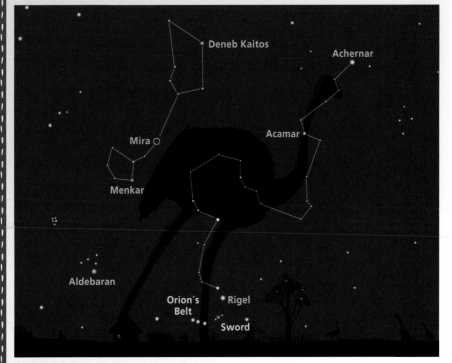

Eridanus the River, shown early in the evening, looking east, and appearing as an ostrich.

The eastern sky at a glance

Beautiful Orion, with its impressive red giant star, Betelgeuse, and blue supergiant star, Rigel, is centred in the eastern sky. These stars frame Orion's famous Belt and misty M42. Lemon-yellow Procyon is just rising in the east, so any dust in the atmosphere will give it a ruddy hue. It marks the lower star in a stunning arc of starlight including twin orange stars Aldebaran and Betelgeuse. Sirius, the brightest star in the night sky, blazes prominently in the east-southeast, while Capella looms low in the northeastern sky. Canopus nearly matches its height in the southeast. Mira (if it is visible) may burn prominently overhead.

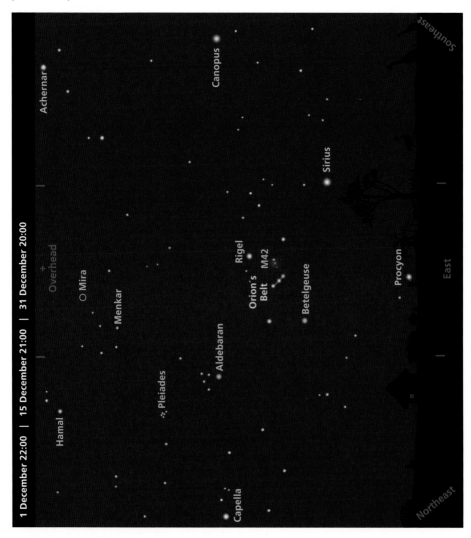

The western sky at a glance

The mid-western sky is pretty barren, save for the faint Y-shaped star pattern of the Aquarius Water Jar and the Circlet of Pisces. The Great Square of Pegasus lies in the mid-northwestern sky, while the Horse's nose (Enif) is beginning to sniff the horizon. Fomalhaut is the solitary beacon of the western celestial landscape, unless a bright planet burns more prominently along the zodiac – from Hamal in Aries, through the Circlet of Pisces and the Water Jar of Aquarius to the Paper Boat of Capricornus, which has touched the west-southwestern horizon and will soon be setting.

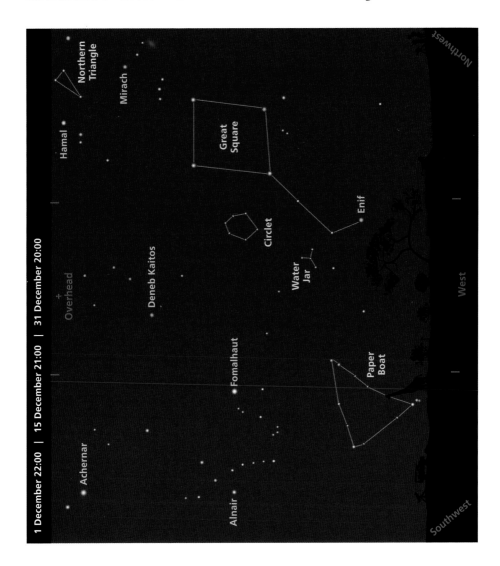

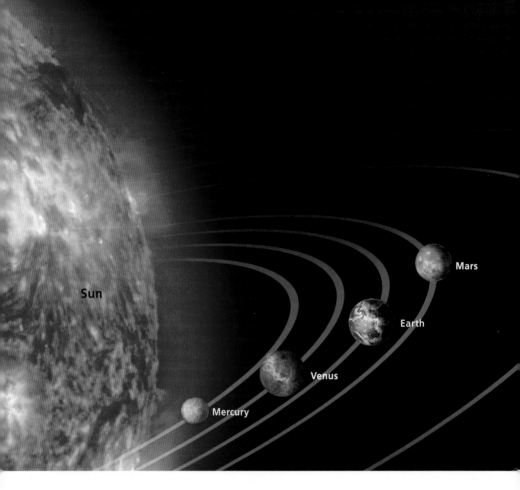

Sun

Mercury

Venus

Earth

Mars

OUR SOLAR SYSTEM

The solar system is a family of objects orbiting our star, the Sun. It contains eight planets (including Earth), several dwarf planets (including Pluto) and small solar system bodies (including comets) too numerous to count.

Dwarf planets are too small and faint to be seen without a telescope. Of the small solar system bodies, comets occasionally become bright enough to be observed with our naked eyes, and, if we are lucky, we can see them trailing long and graceful tails.

On almost any night, we can also see much smaller solar system debris (dust particles and some larger fragments) burn up in our atmosphere as meteors (shooting stars) or fireballs. On rare occasions, a larger-still chunk of rocky debris can fall to Earth as a meteorite. In this chapter we will take a closer look at these fascinating members of our solar system.

Eight planets orbit the Sun, together with innumerable small solar system bodies.

NASA

The Sun

The Sun is the brightest and closest star in our sky. It is an enormous glowing ball of (mostly) hydrogen gas that measures nearly one and a half million kilometres wide.

Despite its enormity, our Sun is only an average-sized star. The red giant in Orion, Betelgeuse, is nearly 1,000 times larger than our Sun, and there are many stars that are significantly smaller than our Sun.

Did you know?

The brightest and closest star ...
The Sun is so large that you could line up, side by side, more than 2,000 countries the size of Botswana across its middle. Even the Earth is puny in comparison: open the Sun like a cooler box and you could pack nearly one and a half million Earths inside.

If we could move our Sun out to the distance of Alpha Centauri – the closest naked-eye star to our Sun – both stars would appear equal in brightness when seen from Earth.

NASA

It might be the centre of our solar system, but the Sun is simply another star.

Our Sun formed about 4.5 billion years ago from a dense cloud of dust and gas. The cloud (which we call the solar nebula) collapsed, possibly due to the shockwave from a nearby exploding star – called a supernova. As the solar nebula collapsed, most (more than 99%) of the matter was drawn towards the centre to form our Sun. The remaining fragments became a flat swirling disc of material that accumulated into planets and smaller bodies, like moons, asteroids, comets and other debris.

Did you know?

Generations of stars

Astronomers call the Sun a 'second-generation star'. Stars are grouped into generations based on their ages, just like people. First-generation stars were born after the universe formed, and consisted primarily of hydrogen and helium. In the final stages of their lives, however, the most massive of these stars forged heavy metals within their cores, which were ejected into the universe when the stars exploded as supernovae. As our Sun is not old enough to forge heavy metals – although it does contain some – astronomers have concluded that it must have formed from the metal-rich debris expelled by first-generation stars.

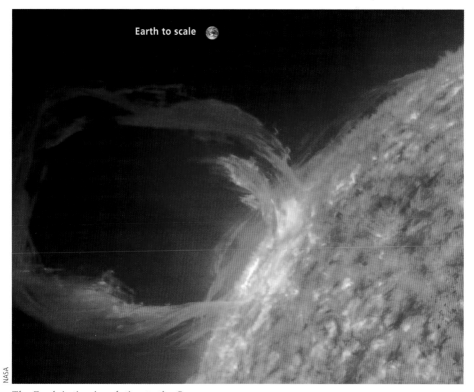

Earth to scale

The Earth is tiny in relation to the Sun.

Light of life

The Sun is the centre of our solar system and the provider of light energy on Earth. Without the Sun, the sky would not have any colour, there would be no breezes, animals would not graze and rains would not fall. All usable energy is directly or indirectly manufactured by the Sun. Plants convert sunlight into food, and humans and animals need plants, air and water to survive. Without the Sun, life on Earth would not exist. It is no wonder that early skywatchers all over the world worshipped the Sun.

Perfect ratio of heat and distance

The Sun's surface is exceedingly hot – approximately 5,500°C, or about four and a half times as hot as molten metal. If the Earth moved closer to the Sun's gaseous surface, it would evaporate immediately. Luckily the Earth is 150 million kilometres away from the Sun, in an orbit where the temperature is 'just right' for us to enjoy its essential light.

Did you know?

Are we there yet?
If you could drive a car from the Earth to the Sun, travelling at 120 kilometres per hour, it would take you about 143 years to get there.

sunspot

Occasionally, when the Sun is near setting (or just rising) and its disc looks so dull that its light is gentler on the eye, visual astronomers can see a naked-eye sunspot – a cooler region that looks like a dark spot on the Sun's face.

Sun lore
How N!iriba made the Sun

Early inhabitants of Botswana saw the Sun *(Letsatsi)* as dependable and predictable – providing light, comfort, guidance and security as it orbited the Earth. With the good, however, also came the bad: the Sun had the power to burn the skin, wither roots and berries, and dry up waterholes. Its scorching heat could inflict hardship during times of drought, forcing hunger, thirst or exhaustion upon the people – or, at times, even sickness and death. Some reasoned the Sun must lie at a great distance, for otherwise it would 'burn people to cinders'.

Early inhabitants of the Central Kalahari believed all things in the sky and on the Earth belonged to N!iriba (also known as Pisiboro) – the enormous supernatural hero of their tales. The beds of the country's rivers were gouged by the magnificent limbs of this giant in his death throes. His decayed flesh became the rivers and his black hair was transformed into rain clouds.

Star lore tells us that N!iriba made the Sun using a korhaan feather, which he shaped into a gentle curve. He tied the feather to a reed, at the end of which was a piece of burning coal from a campfire, held by a cord. Using the coal as a weight, N!iriba tossed his invention into the heavens with a stick, until it sailed so high that it stuck to the starlit sky, providing him with enough daylight to hunt.

More stories of the Sun

Sunset and sunrise explained by the Nyae Nyae !Kung

The Nyae Nyae !Kung were hunter-gatherers living in Botswana. (Some still live a semblance of this life in the Central Kalahari.) One of their myths tells of a group of people called the !Koa !Koa Kwara (or Knee Knee None), whom they regarded as 'the people who eat the Sun'. The Knee Knee None look like humans but they have no knees and their feet are as thin as blades of grass. They always stand, but sometimes sleep leaning against a tree, which is why they are also known as 'those who sleep standing up'.

The Sun is the Knee Knee None's main source of food. According to the story, the Sun returns to Earth each night in the west, where it turns into an elephant. The elephant is then hunted, killed and eaten by the Knee Knee None. When the sky is blood red at sunset, it is because the Knee Knee None have killed the mighty solar elephant with their spears.

Once they have finished devouring the Sun, one of them takes the animal's collarbone and throws it into the waters of the east beyond their land. By the time morning comes, the bone transforms back into the Sun – it rises out of the water, dries itself in a tree (until it is bright and yellow), then begins its daily journey across the sky, repeating the cycle of life, death and rebirth.

Each day at sunset, the Sun turns into an elephant, which the Knee Knee None kill with their spears, the animal's blood turning the sky red.

The watchful eye of the Sun

Many of the myths about the Sun incorporate the belief that the Sun moved back under the Earth to rise again the following day. The Basarwa accepted that, after setting, the Sun moved back under the Earth to rise again in the east.

Other tales said that the Sun moved to the east by returning over the top of the stone dome of the sky at night; this dome was also surrounded by water. The stone had tiny holes in it, so, as the Sun moved, its light seeped through the holes, creating the stars.

In perhaps one of the most shared, modern-day interpretations of Bantu myth, each time the Sun sets, a giant crocodile on the western edge of the flat Earth swallows the Sun at sunset to ingest its eternal power and energy. It swims, with the Sun burning in its belly, from the eternal waters of the west to the east, where it excretes the Sun, allowing it to rise the next day before being swallowed again.

To some early inhabitants of Botswana, the Sun was the Eye of God, watching over them during the day. Realizing that his people needed rest, God shut his eye at night, allowing darkness to set in. When darkness fell across the land, evil slipped in and corrupt deeds were done – as God was no longer watching.

Did you know?

Crocodiles in myth

The giant crocodile myth bears a remarkable resemblance to the ancient Egyptian myth of the Sun god Ra, who is swallowed each day at sunset by a snake. The Sun passes through the snake's long body, which stretches under the Earth all the way to the east. The Sun exits the snake in the east when it reappears at sunrise.

A visual representation of a crocodile swallowing the Sun at sunset before releasing it the next morning.

Solar and lunar haloes

Sometimes a coloured ring will appear around the Sun or Moon in high clouds after a long stretch of clear days. Through the ages, people have seen this ring as a sign of rain on the way. There is some truth to this belief. This colourful ring – known as a 22° solar or lunar halo – can appear in white, veil-like cirrostratus clouds (some 6–12 kilometres above the ground), which often announce the coming of towering thunderheads. However, if these haloes appear after storms, then a stretch of cool and clear weather may be on its way.

Right: A 22° lunar halo circles the full Moon and slices the constellation Orion at top left.
Below: A 22° solar halo surrounds the Sun, blocked by two fingers held at arm's length.

The Moon

Of all the natural wonders in the night sky, the Moon is the brightest and closest astronomical object to Earth. Many planets have moons, which by definition are astronomical bodies that orbit a planet. Our Moon is approximately 385,000 kilometres away from the Earth. It is the Earth's only natural satellite and shines by reflected sunlight. It is referred to as a 'natural satellite' to differentiate it from artificial satellites, which have been intentionally placed in orbit (such as the International Space Station; see page 175).

The Moon is 3,476 kilometres wide – so wide that Botswana can fit about four times across the Moon's equator.

First lunar mission

On 20 July 1969, Apollo 11 astronaut, Neil Armstrong, first stepped on the Moon – but this was not the first mission to the Moon. On 21 December 1968, Apollo 8 sent humans out of Earth's orbit and into a 20-hour orbit around the Moon, before returning the crew safely back to Earth.

Did you know?

Are we there yet?
If you could drive to the Moon in your car, travelling at about 120 kilometres per hour, the non-stop journey would take you about four months to complete. (It took the astronauts in 1968 only 68 hours to get there, propelled by a rocket.)

The Moon is a natural satellite of the Earth and our closest neighbour in space.

The Moon viewed from space

How did the Moon form?

Our Moon most likely formed by an astronomical object smashing into primordial Earth – when our planet was still semi-molten. That collision threw off huge chunks of molten rock into Earth's orbit. These chunks eventually joined and congealed to form our Moon. The Moon always shows the same face to the Earth, because its orbital period matches its rotational period; every large moon orbiting a planet shares the same fate.

Many moons

Earth is not the only planet with moons: Mars has two moons, Jupiter 79, Saturn 82, Uranus 27 and Neptune 14. Mercury and Venus don't have any moons. Jupiter is the only planet with moons easily visible in handheld binoculars.

Jupiter's moons

Jupiter, the largest planet in our solar system, has four bright moons: Io (I), Europa (E), Ganymede (G) and Callisto (C), in order of distance from the planet. All the moons are visible in 7x binoculars or larger, if you hold the binoculars steady. Their appearance, however, depends on where the moons are in their orbit around Jupiter. As they waltz around Jupiter, their positions shift night after night; sometimes you may not see any moons at all. For more information, go to: **www.skyandtelescope. com/wp-content/observing-tools/jupiter_moons/jupiter.html**.

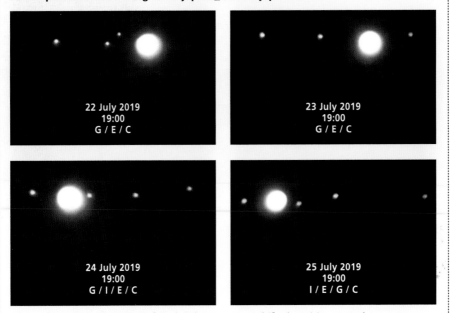

Image showing how Jupiter's four brightest moons shifted position over the course of four nights, viewed at the same time each night. The moons are labelled by their abbreviations, as seen in order from left to right.

Phases of the Moon

The Moon moves through a cycle of changing phases. It takes about 30 days (more or less one month) to complete a single cycle. These lunar phases are a matter of perspective; it all depends on the position from which you are looking at the Moon.

The side of the Moon facing the Sun is always illuminated, while the side facing away from the Sun is always dark because it is in shadow.

Each phase of the Moon is simply described below.

◆ **New Moon** We cannot see the Moon at all during New Moon because the side of the Moon facing the Earth is completely in shadow, with the Sun behind it.

Two views of the Moon: the inner circle diagram shows a view of the Moon from space. The outer circle shows a view of the Moon from Earth.

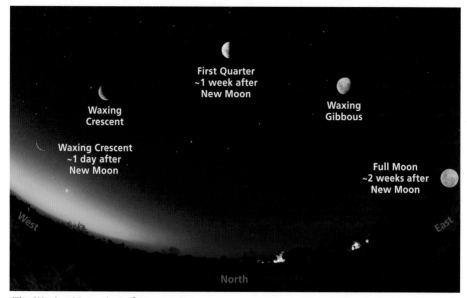

The Waxing Moon (just after sunset).

◆ **Waxing Crescent** The Moon moves in orbit around the Earth. As it moves away from the Sun, we see it as a slender crescent that gradually grows larger and larger. This is referred to as waxing. The waxing phase occurs as the Moon moves away from the Sun, between the times of New Moon and Full Moon.

| 1 Day Before | Full Moon | 1 Day After |

There is only a subtle difference in the Moon's appearance in the days around Full Moon.

◆ **First Quarter** This phase occurs about one week after New Moon. From Earth, we see the Moon is half illuminated so it looks half full. It is always high in the northern sky just after sunset.

◆ **Waxing Gibbous** The waxing Moon after the First Quarter is referred to as gibbous, from the Latin word for 'hump'; more than a semicircle and less than a circle is visible.

◆ **Full Moon** Two weeks after New Moon, the Moon is directly opposite the Sun, its face fully illuminated. Full Moon lasts just an instant, so we rarely see the Moon as really full. Full Moon is bright because all of the exposed surface reflects the Sun. To the untrained eye, Full Moon lasts three days: one day before, Full Moon itself, and one day after.

◆ **Waning Gibbous** After Full Moon, the visible surface begins to reduce. This is referred to as waning until once again the Moon is between the Earth and Sun at New Moon, and the cycle is repeated. The waning phase occurs as the Moon moves towards the Sun, between Full Moon and New Moon.

◆ **Last Quarter** One week after Full Moon, from Earth, the Moon is half illuminated so it looks half full. It is always high in the northern sky just before sunrise.

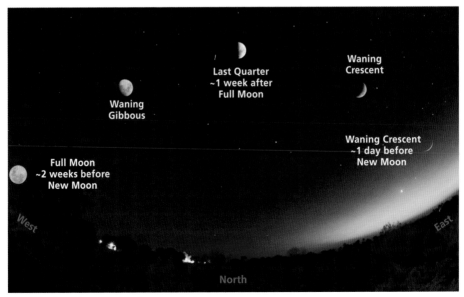

The Waning Moon (just before sunrise).

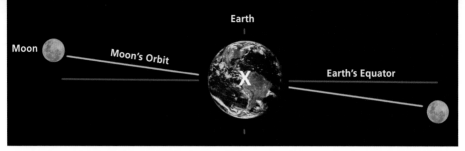

Eclipses only occur when the Moon is at the position labelled 'X' in its orbit. When this happens at New Moon, then a solar eclipse occurs. When it happens at Full Moon, then a lunar eclipse occurs.

Sometimes the Sun or Moon is only partially covered during an eclipse; a partial solar eclipse sequence is shown here.

Solar and lunar eclipses

If the Moon circled the Earth at the same level as our planet's equator, then it would always pass directly in front of the Sun at New Moon. It would block our view of the Sun, causing a solar eclipse.

Continuing this line of thinking, if the Moon stayed in orbit with the equator, then it would also always pass through the centre of Earth's shadow at Full Moon, causing an eclipse of the Moon – or a lunar eclipse.

However, as seen in the illustration at the top of the page, the line of the Moon's orbit is tilted approximately 5° away from the line of the Earth's equator. As a result, eclipses of the Sun and Moon (either partial or total) do occur, but not very often.

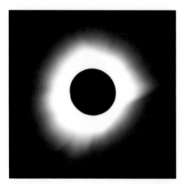

During a total solar eclipse, we can see the black face of the New Moon silhouetted against the Sun's pearly white outer atmosphere. This white wreath or crown surrounding the eclipsed Sun is called a corona.

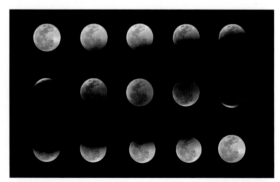

If the Full Moon sails fully through the Earth's shadow, we get a total lunar eclipse, which can turn the Moon blood red. The Nyae Nyae! Kung said that this was caused by a lion putting its paw over the Moon to darken the night – the absence of light being more conducive to hunting.

Earthshine
When the Moon
looks like a crescent,
that shining shape is
created by reflected
sunlight, called
moonlight. The rest of
the Moon's face glows
faintly from reflected
earthlight – this is
called earthshine.

The surface of the Moon

Look at the Moon through binoculars when it is
waxing or waning, as that's when shadows will
enhance the details on its surface, displaying them
in greatest relief. Three main features are visible:

Shadows on the Moon enhance
three features on the surface:
highlands, mountains and seas.

◆ Rugged highlands – these are the Moon's oldest
regions, pitted with uncountable craters.
◆ Smooth and dark maria (Latin for 'seas') – while
skywatchers centuries ago believed they were seas like
those on Earth, they are not. The maria are vast plains
of solidified lava formed early in the Moon's history.
◆ Long chains of mountain ranges – some nearly
rival Mount Everest in height.

Early in the Moon's history, dark basaltic lava (as found along the East African Rift Valley) once
flowed across its surface and pooled inside ancient craters to form dark, smooth maria or seas.

A daylight Moon

The Moon is visible during some daylight hours for about three weeks in every month. It is most noticeable, however, between the First Quarter and the Last Quarter, including the days around Full Moon. It is most difficult to see when it is a crescent within 30° of the Sun, where the sky is brightest and the Moon thinnest.

Although we associate the Moon with the dark night sky, the Moon is bright enough to be visible in broad daylight.

Apogee and perigee

The Moon does not move around the Earth in a perfect circle – it has an elliptical (oval-shaped) orbit, so sometimes the Moon is closer to Earth. When the Moon is closest to the Earth (perigee), it lies about 360,000 kilometres away. When it is farthest away (apogee), it is about 400,000 kilometres distant.

Perigee   Apogee

The Moon appears about 25% larger at perigee than at apogee, creating a visually spectacular supermoon, especially when rising.

Moon lore

Basarwa Moon tales

The early people of Botswana named the Moon *ngwedi*. The Setswana word for month *(kgwedi)* is similar; this suggests that these early skywatchers were among the many cultures who used the Moon's cycle as a way to keep track of passing time. To some early people of the Kalahari, the great supernatural hero Pisiboro (discussed in the Sun section on page 147) created the Moon from a //ha root (a food source for the local population). After devouring most of the root (except for a sliver), the giant tossed it high into the sky with its climbing vine still attached. The vine climbed so high that it stuck to the sky, where it took root as the Moon. The same people who ate the Sun (in a legend told by the Nyae Nyae !Kung on page 148) also ate the Moon. The story goes that the Moon turns into an eland when it sets in the west. It is said that the Knee Knee None ate the eland Moon, then threw its collarbone into the waters of the east. The bone transformed back into the Moon, ready to rise once again the next night.

In Nyae Nyae !Kung lore, if the Moon appeared extremely red, it was a sign that someone had died, or that some great animal had succumbed to the hunt – including the eland to the Knee Knee None.

/Kaggen makes moonlight

A story tells us that the Moon was made by the cheeky creator, /Kaggen, who could transform himself into any animal, particularly an eland. The eland symbolized spiritual and environmental well-being and embodied supernatural energy. When /Kaggen's children killed this beloved creature, he took the carcass and pierced its gallbladder with a stick. Spray shot into his eyes, blinding him and creating night. Dismayed, he swept the ground with his hands, seeking something to wipe his eyes with. To his delight, he found an ostrich feather. After wiping his eyes, he threw the soiled feather into the sky, where it became the Moon, providing him with light.

More stories of the Moon

/Kaggen's sandal

/Kaggen walked across the hot Kalahari sands, until he felt tired. He thrust his hot, tired feet into a pool of water, but this awakened the water spirit who flew into a rage and froze the water solid, locking his sandals in ice. /Kaggen pounded the ice with his fists, until he broke free a block of ice that contained one of his sandals, but he could not shake it free from the ice. Enraged, /Kaggen tossed the ice block (with his sandal) into the night sky, where it became the Moon. The dark region we see with our unaided eyes is his sandal, while the bright portion is the block of ice clinging to it.

Woman and child

Some early Botswana inhabitants imagined the Moon's dark patches as a woman carrying a child; the woman was placed on the Moon as a punishment for gathering firewood when she should have been helping others prepare for a festival honouring their spirit ancestors. To this day, the woman and child remain visible on the Moon, serving as a warning to others who might repeat the deed.

A jealous Sun

A tale is told in |Xam mythology that when the Sun saw the magnificence of the Full Moon, it became jealous. To stop the Moon from getting any brighter, the Sun acted quickly; using its sharp rays like a knife, the Sun began slicing the Moon into ever-smaller bits.

When the Moon was almost gone, he begged the Sun to stop and consider his children who loved him. After giving the matter some thought, the Sun agreed, on one condition: the Moon, when full, could not outshine the Sun. The Moon agreed, but the Sun still did not trust him. That is why, after every Full Moon, the Sun continues to carve away at the Moon, leaving only a backbone from which the Moon can regrow.

The Moon is characterized in different ways in traditional star lore: from a sandal, to a mother and child, to an object of jealous rage.

The lunar fertility cycle and the transforming Moon

Each month, the Basarwa saw the Moon change its shape in a rhythmic cycle. After the invisible 'Baboon Moon', a slender crescent appeared in the western sky just after sunset. This was seen as a male form of the Moon.

For a week, the crescent grew fatter and fatter, while moving higher and higher into the sky. At Half Moon, the male began its mystical transformation into a female. As the nights progressed, the woman's belly would swell larger and larger – until Full Moon, when she rose fully pregnant in the east after sunset.

The cycle then reversed itself, with the woman's belly shrinking until the Last Quarter was visible in the dawn sky, when it transformed back into a male. In this way, the Basarwa saw the Moon give birth to itself. The Setswana word for Moon (*kgwedi*) also means menstruation, acknowledging the link between the Moon and the fertility cycle.

According to the Basarwa, the Moon could be male or female, depending on its phase.

The G/wi Moon-cloak

The G/wi are a small Basarwa society from central Botswana. They believe that the Moon is a man who hunts late into New Moon. He feeds the meat to his family, then makes a cloak out of the skin, which he uses to cover himself on New Moon night. He cannot be seen. His wife, who has no cloak, grows cold. Night by night, she gradually pulls the cloak away from her husband until he has none of it; this is now Full Moon. Slowly he takes it back again – until he has it all. By this time his children are hungry and they go to their father and eat the cloak just before New Moon. So the hunter must go out again to find food to feed his family, starting the cycle anew.

The Moon is a man who hunts and covers himself in an invisible cloak.

The G/wi people of central Botswana tell a tale of the lunar phases as a husband and wife battling over possession of a warm Moon-cloak.

The planets

Our solar system has two types of planets: terrestrial planets and gas giants. Moving outward in order from the Sun, first we have the four terrestrial planets: Mercury, Venus, Earth and Mars. These are followed by the four gas giant planets: Jupiter, Saturn, Uranus and Neptune.

We call the inner planets terrestrial, from the Latin word *terra*, meaning 'Earth'. All terrestrial planets are made primarily of rock and metal. We call the outer planets gas giants because they are enormous spheres of mainly hydrogen and helium gas, with a metal or rocky core.

From Earth, we can see only five of the planets with the unaided eye: Mercury, Venus, Mars, Jupiter and Saturn. All these planets shine by reflected light from the Sun. Some people with keen eyesight have also seen Uranus, but that feat requires precise knowledge of where to look among the multitude of stars, as it is so dim.

3rd Rock from the Sun

Earth is the third planet from the Sun and it is also a rocky planet, so we say that Earth is the 'third rock from the Sun', which was also the name of a television series popular in the late 1990s.

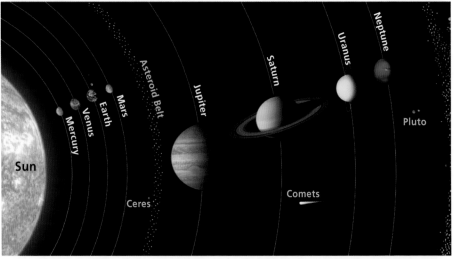

Our solar system features eight planets: four inner rocky or terrestrial planets (those to the left of the Asteroid Belt) and four outer gas giant planets (those between the Asteroid Belt and Pluto, which has been demoted to a dwarf planet). The Asteroid Belt is a 'failed planet'. The largest body in the Asteroid Belt is Ceres, which, like Pluto, is a dwarf planet. The eight major planets orbit the Sun in a counterclockwise direction along a similar plane, but at different distances from the Sun. Comets travel in random orbits and visit from afar.

Scaling the Sun

The distances from the Sun are not accurately demonstrated in the illustrations on this page. We would need a very big piece of paper if we wanted to depict the planets' distances from the Sun to scale. For example, if the Sun was drawn the size of a tennis ball, then Neptune, the farthest planet, would be drawn about 25 kilometres away from the edge of the illustrated Sun.

The relative sizes of the planets: the numbers in brackets are each planet's diameter in kilometres.

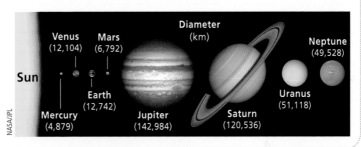

Sizing up the planets

The planets vary in size, with Jupiter being the largest and Mercury the smallest. Earth and Venus, and Uranus and Neptune, are often referred to as sister planets because they share similar characteristics such as size, mass and composition.

Orbital racetrack

All the planets are orbiting the Sun according to their own schedule. All these orbits form a 'cosmic racetrack' around the Sun. The closer a planet is to the Sun, the faster it orbits the Sun.

The distance of each planet from the Sun is shown in millions of kilometres.

The length of time it takes each planet to orbit the Sun is given in parentheses: the closer a planet is to the Sun, the faster it orbits the Sun.

How did the planets form?

As mentioned in the section about the Sun, scientists think that a giant star, close to where the Sun is today, exploded about 4.6 million years ago, sending shock waves slamming into a cloud of dust and gas.

Once disturbed, the cloud began to spin and forces flattened it out into a disc. The spinning motion drew dust and gas into the disc's centre, where it condensed into the Sun. Most of the remaining dust particles in the cloud began to clump together through gentle collisions to make more solid particles, which gently collided with more particles until they eventually grew into the planets and other solar system bodies. The gas giants most likely formed because the cores were massive enough, and far enough away from the Sun's heat to be icy enough, for their gravity to attract most of the remaining gas in the spinning disc, including the remaining hydrogen and helium gases that pervaded the cloud. Gravity is the force that attracts two bodies. The more massive a body, the stronger its gravitational pull, and the more matter it can collect.

Right: Scientists hypothesize that a giant star close to the Sun exploded 4.6 million years ago, leading to the formation of our solar system. **Below:** It took a few million years for the solar system's family of planets to form after the original explosion of a giant star.

NASA

NASA

The leftover debris

There are still chunks of dust, rock and ice left over from the formation of the planets. Most of these 'leftovers' or remaining solar system bodies are too small to be called planets; rather they are divided into dwarf planets, asteroids (minor planets), comets, meteoroids, meteors and meteorites.

Dwarf planets

Dwarf planets are circular bodies that orbit the Sun beyond Neptune, except for Ceres, which orbits the Sun in the Asteroid Belt (described below). Unlike the eight planets that orbit the Sun along clear paths, most dwarf planets share their orbits with a multitude of other celestial bodies. Over 200 dwarf planets may exist in our solar system; the most popular one known is Pluto. All dwarf planets are too faint to be seen with unaided eyes.

Pluto, the dwarf planet, compared to the Earth. This image was created to demonstrate the size difference between the two worlds. (Note that Pluto is not in such close proximity to the Earth.)

Asteroids (minor planets)

These minor planets are small, airless, rocky bodies of irregular shape. Most asteroids orbit the Sun in a belt that lies between the orbits of Mars and Jupiter – this is called the Asteroid Belt. If all the asteroids in the Belt were combined into a ball, they would still be much smaller than the Earth's Moon. The largest asteroid in this Belt is Vesta, which is 525 kilometres wide. Asteroids are too faint to be seen with unaided eyes, though Vesta may, on occasion, become just bright enough to be glimpsed, if one knows exactly where to look. As mentioned earlier, the dwarf planet called Ceres also lies within the Asteroid Belt.

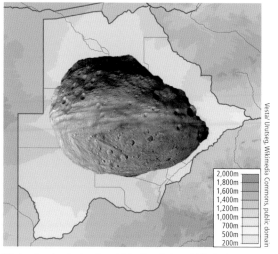

Vesta, the largest asteroid in the Asteroid Belt, is about three-fifths the size of Botswana.

Comets

Comets are remnants of rock and ice from the extremely cold, outer regions of the solar system. Most lie in a vast cloud of comets known as the Oort Cloud. A comet's solid body (or nucleus) ranges in size from less than 1 kilometre in diameter to as much as 300 kilometres in diameter. The comet body at left (67P/Churyumov–Gerasimenko) is only about 3 kilometres across, meaning it could fit on Maun's airstrip.

Most comets travel in highly elliptical orbits, bringing them close to the Sun before taking them far away. Some comets enter our solar system then leave and never return.

Top left: This image of the nucleus of Comet 67P/Churyumov-Gerasimenko superimposed above Maun's airstrip shows they are of a similar size.

Left: As a comet approaches the Sun, ice can erupt jets of gas which, along with any dust, form a temporary atmosphere around the solid nucleus.

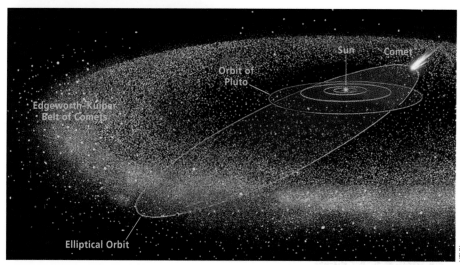

Most comets originate in the Oort Cloud and travel in highly elliptical or cigar-shaped orbits. Some comets reside in the Edgeworth–Kuiper belt, a doughnut-shaped region of icy bodies beyond the orbit of Neptune.

A constant stream of charged particles from the Sun (called solar wind) blows the fine material in the comet's atmosphere into a long tail, the dusty part of which shines by reflected sunlight, as shown in the image to the right. Comets are highly unpredictable, but when a bright one appears, it can shine magnificently in the night sky.

There is a website that lists and charts the comets that can be seen with unaided eyes or binoculars. Visit **www.heavens-above.com**. Unlike meteors or 'shooting stars' that streak across the sky in a flash, comets can be visible to unaided eyes or with binoculars for days or months; they move slowly against the backdrop of the stars, night after night.

On 24 December 2011, NASA astronaut Dan Burbank captured this image of Comet C/2011 W3 (Lovejoy) from the International Space Station. As a comet nears the Sun, it can form a long dust tail that we see illuminated by sunlight.

NASA

Comet 46P/Wirtanen

This composite image shows the movement of Comet 46P/Wirtanen, near the Pleiades star cluster, on the nights of 15 and 16 December 2018. On these nights, the comet made a historic and close pass by Earth – which is why the comet appeared to move so much over the course of one night. Most comets are much farther away and don't appear to move as much. When closest, the comet was about 11 million kilometres from Earth – or roughly the distance it would take to make 30 trips to the Moon, which is close by astronomical standards.

15 December 2018

16 December 2018

Comet 46P/Wirtanen, near the Pleiades star cluster.

Meteoroids and meteors

A meteoroid is a small particle in space – smaller than an asteroid, and most likely broken off from a comet or asteroid orbiting the Sun. Untold millions of meteoroids enter the Earth's atmosphere every day; when this happens, it's called a meteor.

Meteors that burn up high in the atmosphere are commonly known as 'shooting stars', appearing as streaks of light as they enter the atmosphere. As the meteorite plunges deep into the atmosphere (moving at about 70 kilometres per second), friction heats up the surrounding air, causing the meteoroid and the particles in its wake to glow.

Extremely bright meteors, reaching magnitudes of –4 (like Venus) or brighter, are called fireballs. Fireballs about as bright as a Full Moon, or brighter, explode in the atmosphere, and are called bolides. Some bolide explosions are accompanied by a sonic boom – the noise created when an object travels faster than the speed of sound. About 5,000 bolides occur per year, but very few of these are actually observed.

Antlion

Myrmeleontidae (antlion) larva.
The !Kung believed falling stars turned into antlions, commonly found in the Kalahari sands. The larvae of these ant-eating insects trap their prey in cone-shaped tunnels.

Meteor showers

As the Earth journeys around the Sun, it sometimes crosses a comet's orbit, littered with rocky debris. The Earth collides with the debris, creating a meteor shower. Meteor showers are predictable because Earth passes through these comet debris streams at the same time each year. Viewed from Earth, the meteors appear to rain down (shower) from a single area in the sky called the radiant.

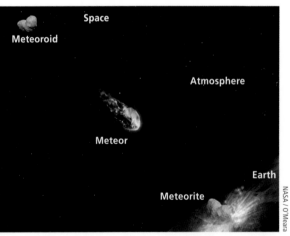

NASA / O'Meara

Small particles in space change name depending on where they are in relation to the Earth: meteoroids are particles in space; meteors are particles in the Earth's atmosphere; and meteorites are particles that have reached the Earth's surface.

Did you know?

Meteor showers

The radiant, or apparent point of origin, of a meteor shower is an illusion. When seen from space, meteors travel through the Earth's atmosphere in parallel paths. But when seen from the Earth, meteors appear to shoot out from a single point in the sky.

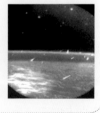

NASA photo of a meteor shower called The Leonids, as viewed from space.

Botswana's best meteor showers

These showers are named after the constellations in which their radiant lies. The dates given are peak activity times for meteor viewing in southern Africa. The meteor counts are a conservative range of average numbers that a single observer might expect to see after spending an hour under the stars. There is no set direction in which to look – they can occur anywhere in the sky.

April Lyrids (21–24 April) A few fast, white meteors with occasional fireballs.

Eta Aquarids (7, 8 May) A dependable shower producing one to ten very swift meteors with long paths. These meteors are fragments of Halley's Comet.

Alpha Scorpiids (16 May) A weak but unusual shower that produces long fireballs bright enough to be seen in the daytime. Look after sunset into the early evening.

Southern Delta Aquarids (28, 29 July) One swift meteor every five or so minutes.

Perseids (11–13 August) Visible very low in the northern sky for just a few hours before sunrise. You may see a few colourful fireballs, even in the morning twilight.

Orionids (20–21 October) Two to five very fast meteors per hour, with the occasional fireball. These meteors are also related to Halley's Comet.

Taurids (9–10 October; 11–12 November) This meteor shower has two peaks. The 9–10 October peak is best for southern hemisphere viewers; the 11–12 November peak favours northern hemisphere observers. However, meteors from both showers can be viewed throughout the month-long period from both hemispheres. It is especially common to see what are known as 'Halloween Fireballs', which can be very brilliant and a real treat at this festive time of year.

Leonids (16–17 November) Two to ten very fast meteors per hour, on these given dates, between the 'showstopper' years. Every 33 years, a showstopper happens, during which innumerable meteors (a true shower) fall from the sky for a brief period. The last showstopper years occurred on these given dates from 1998–2001.

Geminids (12–14 December) Three to 15 fast, yellow meteors per hour, many of which are bright. Considered the year's most consistent and reliable shower.

Most meteor showers are named for either the constellation or star from which they appear to radiate. For instance, the Delta Aquariid meteor shower tells us that trails of shooting stars belonging to this shower can be traced back to a point near the star called Delta Aquarii. A simple internet search will point you to sites that give times and dates of meteor showers. Occasionally, you'll see a sporadic meteor within a meteor shower – it cannot be traced back to a radiant.

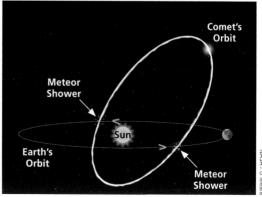

Meteor showers occur when the Earth collides with debris in a comet's orbit.

Observing a meteor or meteor shower

Stargazers should plan to spend a fair amount of time under the night sky if they wish to see meteors or meteor showers. Generally, a handful of meteors can be seen in one hour. True meteor showers – when meteors appear to rain down from the sky – are rare. Most meteor showers are best observed after midnight and before sunrise, as the Earth faces the oncoming stream of particles.

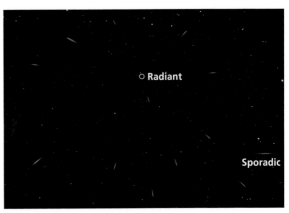

This illustration shows how a meteor shower rains down from the radiant; at right, a sporadic meteor moves on its own trajectory, which cannot be traced back to the radiant.

Meteorite fragments recovered in Botswana

On 2 June 2018, astronomers spotted a 3-metre, table-sized asteroid approaching Earth. They named it 2018 LA. Eight hours later, travelling at a speed of 16 kilometres per second, it entered the Earth's atmosphere, creating a spectacular bolide that exploded in the upper atmosphere, turning night briefly into day over much of southern Africa. The shockwave generated by the event resulted in a series of sonic booms strong enough to rattle structures and alarm the staff at Dinaka Safari Camp in the Central Kalahari Game Reserve. The explosion shattered the asteroid and pieces of it fell to Earth to become fully fledged meteorites. Peter Jenniskens, a meteor expert of the NASA-sponsored SETI Institute in California, calculated the landing area of the meteorite. He worked with Esko Lyytinen and Jarmo Moilanen of the Finnish Fireball Network to recover the myriad fragments.

Meteorites are protected under Botswana law, meaning that the Botswana National Museum is responsible for curating all the samples recovered. Investigations into meteorite fragments are coordinated by the Botswana Geoscience Institute (BGI).

This is only the third time an asteroid has been detected before striking the Earth's atmosphere, and it is the second time meteorite fragments have been recovered. The first pre-strike detection was on 7 October 2008, when a 4-metre asteroid exploded over Sudan (2008 TC3). By the end of 2008, meteorite fragments weighing a total of about 5 kilograms were recovered from the Nubian Desert.

The second asteroid detection took place in 2014 and was known as 2014 AA. The roughly 3-metre asteroid entered Earth's atmosphere about

This tiny fragment, believed to be part of the meteorite called 2018 LA, was recovered in the Central Kalahari Game Reserve, Botswana, in June 2018.

Meteorites

A meteorite is a meteoroid that travels through the Earth's atmosphere (when it becomes a meteor) and hits the Earth's surface (when it becomes a meteorite). Every 2,000 years or so, a meteorite about the size of a football field hits the Earth, causing significant damage.

Only once every few million years a meteorite large enough to threaten Earth's civilization comes along; impact craters on Earth, the Moon and other planetary bodies are evidence of these fantastic collisions.

Botswana's meteorite craters

◆ **Kgagodi** (GPS coordinates: 27° 35' East; 22° 29' South) The 3.4 kilometre-wide Kgagodi Basin is in eastern Botswana, approximately 7 kilometres south of Kgagodi Village. It was first recognized in 1997 during the course of a water drilling project. In 2002, Dion Brandt, of the Impact Cratering Research Group (at the University of the Witwatersrand in Johannesburg, South Africa), and colleagues confirmed it to be a meteorite impact structure dating back to between 65 and 180 million years ago.

21 hours after Richard Kowalski (of a near-Earth asteroid search program in the United States) discovered the object only 500,000 kilometres from Earth and approaching fast. Peter Brown, a scientist from the University of Ontario, Canada, then used data from extremely low-frequency (infrasound) detectors — maintained to pinpoint the location of any powerful detonation, including airbursts from incoming meteors — to determine that the space rock exploded in the atmosphere about 3,000 kilometres east of Caracas, Venezuela. Asteroid 2014 AA was too small to reach the ground intact.

Did you know?

The University of Helsinki Report on 2018 LA
The first meteorite was found after five days of walking and scouring around [the Central Kalahari Game Reserve] by a team of geoscientists from Botswana International University of Science & Technology (BIUST), Botswana Geoscience Institute (BGI) and University of Botswana's Okavango Research Institute (ORI). The Department of Wildlife and National Parks granted access and deployed park rangers for protection and participation in the search.

Jenniskens, who travelled to Botswana to assist in the search, teamed up with Oliver Moses (from ORI), to gather security surveillance videos in Rakops and Maun, to get better constraints on the position and altitude of the fireball's explosion. Professor Alexander Proyer, from BIUST, led the joint expedition while Mohutsiwa Gabadirwe, BGI senior curator, coordinated access to the protected fall area in the game reserve. Professor Roger Gibson, Head of Geosciences at the University of the Witwatersrand in Johannesburg, South Africa, also assisted in locating the fall area. The meteorite was eventually spotted by BIUST geologist, Lesedi Seitshiro.

This spans the age of the dinosaurs, and could be related to their mass extinction 65 million years ago. It is the first impact structure recognized in the region of the Kalahari Desert in southern Africa.

◆ **Okavango Delta I** (GPS coordinates: 19° 07' 40.0" South; 23° 18' 12.7" East) Hidden in the Okavango Delta lies what is possibly another meteorite crater. It is marked by a circular region, measuring about 18 kilometres across, that is visible only in aerial magnetic data. It is not visible on Google Earth or in normal satellite imagery, as the crater appears to be buried beneath about 200 to 500 metres of sediment.

The Kgagodi crater (Google Earth image).

◆ **Okavango Delta II** (GPS coordinates: 19° 49' 13.8" South; 23° 07' 10.25" East) In 1994, Colin Henshaw of the British Astronomical Association came to Botswana as a science teacher. A year earlier, he learned of a possible meteorite crater close to Maun. Henshaw heard two conflicting tales of its origins. In the first version, local residents recall a fireball event during the 1930s. The second version tells of a fireball and seismic event on 12 August 1978 at 12:30 local time (unknown whether it was day or night). Henshaw put together an expedition with his students and a local guide to explore the site. They found the crater to be 'perfectly circular and saucer-shaped' with a 'very slightly raised rim'. It measured roughly 22 metres wide and 4 metres deep. He and his students swept the area for fragments but found none.

Okavango Delta II (Google Earth image).

The crater's discovery remains a mystery – so does its origin. It could be a sinkhole, excavation site, depression left behind by bombs discarded after the war with Angola during the 1970s, or the impact site of a meteorite. If it did come from outer space, the impactor had to be small, perhaps 2 metres in diameter, and may lie buried below the surface. If it is a genuine meteorite crater, Henshaw suggests that the site be preserved (especially as it is in a conservation area), as it may serve as a tourist attraction.

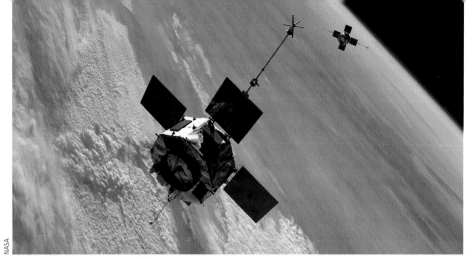

NASA

Two satellites photographed in space orbit the Earth.

Earth's artificial Moons

There are many artificial satellites orbiting Earth. Although they have the appearance of a star, they move at a steady pace across the night sky. This makes it easy to differentiate them from other objects such as aircraft (which have blinking lights) or meteors (which move much faster). The most common types of satellites orbiting the Earth include communication satellites, weather satellites, Earth observation satellites (for scientists and others interested in observing the Earth), navigation satellites, space stations and space telescopes. There is also a lot of orbital debris up there, including spent rocket boosters, defunct satellites, debris from collisions or explosions, and other 'junk'.

Like the Moon, artificial satellites shine by reflected sunlight. Sometimes satellites tumble in orbit, causing erratic fluctuations in brightness as they cross the sky. If a satellite enters Earth's shadow, it begins to redden (just as the Sun does when it nears the horizon). It also gradually fades as it plunges deeper and deeper into shadow, until it vanishes from view. People often mistake this remarkable sight for a UFO jetting off into outer space.

Above: The author used a long exposure to capture the trails left by two satellites as they moved across the night sky.
Right: Long exposure showing the reddening of a satellite trail and how it fades when it enters the Earth's shadow.

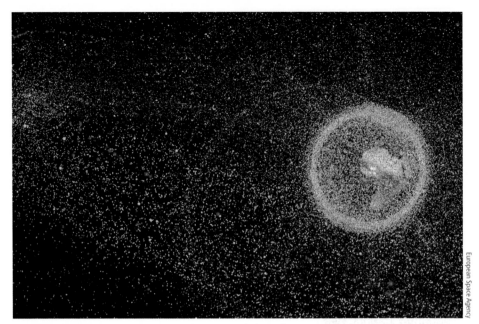

This European Space Agency image shows actual data of space junk around Earth.

Space junk

Since the Soviet Union launched the first artificial satellite in 1957 (called Sputnik), more than 8,950 artificial satellites have been placed into Earth's orbit. About 5,000 are still in space; only about 1,950 are operational today. The remaining satellites are floating around above the Earth, along with the roughly 5,450 spent rockets and boosters that propelled them into orbit. The informal name for this motley assortment is 'space junk' – floating metal corpses no longer of value.

More than 500 of these objects have either broken up, collided with one another or exploded in orbit, creating even more space junk, the total mass of which weighs more than 8,400 tonnes. Some 34,000 pieces larger than 10 centimetres are in orbit; some 900,000 bits measure 1–10 centimetres in diameter; and about 128 million fragments are smaller than 1 centimetre in diameter. The number of debris objects regularly tracked by Space Surveillance Networks and maintained in their catalogue is only about 22,300.

In November 2008, an astronaut accidentally lost a tool bag while working on the International Space Station. The bag began orbiting the Earth as space junk until it burned up in Earth's atmosphere as a meteor, nearly a year later.

The International Space Station (ISS)

The biggest and brightest operational satellite orbiting Earth is the football field-sized International Space Station (ISS). Travelling at a speed of approximately 28,000 kilometres per hour, or about 8 kilometres per second, the Station orbits Earth every 90 minutes at an average altitude of approximately 370 kilometres. The ISS is clearly seen when it passes high overhead at night. Sometimes it is the brightest object in the night sky aside from the Moon and Venus.

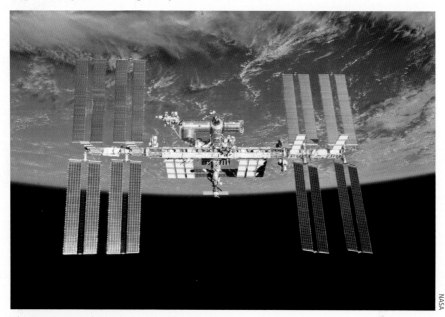

The International Space Station orbits Earth.

Did you know?

Track the Space Station
To find out when the ISS passes overhead, visit **www.heavens-above.com**.
Search for and enter the observing location, then click on the ISS link under the 'Satellites' sub-heading: 10-day predictions for satellites of special interest.

This long-exposure photograph shows the International Space Station leaving a bright trail in the night skies above Botswana.

References for star lore

Alcock, P.G. *Venus Rising*. http://assa.saao.ac.za/astronomy-in-south-africa/ethnoastronoy/venus-rising/.

Bleek, W.H.I. 1875. *A Brief Account of Bushman Folklore*. Trubner & Co., London.

Bleek, W.H.I. & Lloyd, L.C. 1911. *Specimens of Bushman Folklore*. G. Allen Publishing, London.

Clegg, A. 1986. Some Aspects of Tswana Cosmology. *Botswana Notes and Records* 18: 33-37.

Dacke, M. *et al*. 2013. Dung Beetles Use the Milky Way for Orientation. *Current Biology* 24 January.

David, G.A. 2013. *The Kivas of Heaven*. Adventures Unlimited Press, Illinois.

Guenther, M.G. 1999. *Tricksters and Trancers: Bushman Religion and Society*. Indiana University Press, Bloomington.

Jonsson, U. 1988. *Stars Over Botswana*. UPUB, Botswana.

Laney, D. 2017. *African Starlore*. www.beforebc.de/AfricanaResources/AfricanaResources/AfricanStarlore.html.

Leeuw, L.L. 2007. Setswana Astronomical Nomenclature. *African Skies* 11: 17.

Lloyd, L.C. 1889. *Short Account of Further Bushman Material Collected*. Presented to both Houses of the Parliament of the Cape of Good Hope. David Nutt, London.

Lynch, P.A. 2004. *African Mythology A to Z*. Facts on File, New York.

Marshall, L.J. 1975. Two Jũ/wã Constellations. *Botswana Notes and Records* 7: 153-159.

Marshall, L.J. 2004. Nyae Nyae !Kung Beliefs and Rites. Peabody Museum Monographs 8. Peabody Museum Press, Cambridge.

Snedegar, K.V. 1995. Stars and Seasons in Southern Africa. *Vistas in Astronomy* 39: 529-539.

Snyman, M., Ntuli, B. & Ntuli, D. 2006. *The Crocodile who Swallows the Sun and Other Stories of the Southern Sky*. Southern Science, Woodhill.

Thompson, G.D. 2007-2018. An Outline Sketch of the Origin and History of Constellations and Star-Names. *South African Star Lore* 6. https://protect-za.mimecast.com/s/SSWOCJZKYAT31nXHVb5P-?domain=members.westnet.com.au.

Vogt, Y. 2012. World's Oldest Ritual Discovered. Worshipped the Python 70,000 Years Ago. www.apollon.uio.no/english/articles/2006/python-english.html.

Vossen and Keuthman (editors). 1986. Some Bushman Star Lore. *Contemporary Studies on Khoisan Part 2*: 169-204. Helmut Buske Verlag, Hamburg.

Warner, B. 1996. Traditional Astronomical Knowledge in Africa. *Astronomy Before the Telescope*. Walker, C. (editor). British Museum Press, London.

Willoughby, W.C. 1928. Some Conclusions Concerning the Bantu Conception of the Soul. *Journal of the International African Institute* 1: 338-347.

Glossary

apogee point in the Moon's orbit when it is farthest from the Earth; also applies to satellites.

asterism familiar grouping of stars that is not a constellation; the Big Dipper is an asterism in the Ursa Major constellation.

asteroid small, rocky object (larger than a meteoroid and smaller than a planet) that orbits the Sun.

averted vision observing technique used by amateur astronomers; involves looking slightly to one side of a faint object, so its light falls on the eye's night-sensitive part of the retina; same as peripheral vision.

azimuth direction of a celestial object measured clockwise in degrees around the observer's horizon from the north – with due north 0°, due east 90°, due south 180° and due west 270°; another name for the compass points.

black hole collapsed core of a massive star whose gravitational pull is so strong that not even light can escape.

bolide meteor as bright as the Full Moon or brighter; often explodes with audible sonic boom.

Ceres dwarf planet that orbits the Sun in the Asteroid Belt.

comet icy rocks (leftover debris from formation of solar system) from outer regions of solar system.

cone cells light-sensitive cells in the eye responsible for daytime/colour vision.

constellation one of 88 officially recognized groups of stars that, when seen from Earth, forms a pattern in an area of sky with boundaries.

corona means crown; the diaphanous outermost part of the Sun's atmosphere visible during a total solar eclipse.

crater a depression from the impact of a natural object from interplanetary space with Earth or with other comparatively large solid bodies, like the Moon.

double star pair of stars that appear close to one another in the sky; some revolve around one another (binary stars); others just appear close together from the Earth because they are both in the same line of sight (optical doubles).

dwarf planet object orbiting the Sun that is big and heavy enough to resemble a planet, but not big enough to 'clear' a free path on its orbit. Since 2006, Pluto has been reclassified as a dwarf planet. The largest asteroid, Ceres, has also been reclassified as a dwarf planet.

Earth third planet from the Sun and largest terrestrial planet. Also our home planet, it is the only known planet to harbour life.

earthshine pale glow on unlit part of the Moon caused by light reflected from Earth.

eclipse when a celestial object obscures the light from another celestial object, such as when the Moon blocks light from the Sun (solar eclipse), or the Earth's shadow falls on the Moon (lunar eclipse).

ecliptic imaginary line on the sky that marks the annual path of the Sun, Moon and planets; also called the zodiac.

Edgeworth–Kuiper Belt flat ring of small icy bodies that orbit the Sun beyond the orbit of Neptune.

equator imaginary line drawn around the Earth, equally distant from the north and south poles; the latitude line of 0°.

fireball meteor generally brighter than magnitude –4 (rough magnitude of Venus).

fovea central area within the retina of the eye.

Full Moon point in the Moon's orbit when it is opposite the Sun as seen from Earth; at this time the Moon is fully illuminated by the Sun.

galactic bulge spherical core of a galaxy, containing swarms of stars.

galaxy huge collection of gas, dust and billions of stars and their solar systems, held together by gravity.

gas giant (planet) large planet in the outer solar system, composed mostly of hydrogen and helium gas, with an Earth-sized solid or semisolid core. Our solar system has four gas giant planets: Jupiter, Saturn, Uranus and Neptune.

gibbous phase of the Moon between half and full, from the Latin word for 'hump'; more than a semicircle and less than a circle of the Moon is visible.

globular cluster spherical group of up to a million stars held together by gravity; these remote objects orbit the central regions of galaxies out to great distances and consist of old stars.

halo (22°) circular colourful ring around the Moon or Sun caused by light passing through ice crystals in the sky.

halo (galactic) a massive component of a galaxy that can extend beyond a distance of 100,000 light years from the centre, primarily made up of globular clusters and a scattering of old individual stars.

highlands light areas on the Moon, old and heavily cratered.

hypergiant most massive star type in the universe; it is extremely unstable and thus short-lived.

Jupiter fifth planet from the Sun; largest planet in our solar system; gas giant.

light pollution unnatural brightening of the night sky caused by street lights and other artificial light sources; has a disruptive effect on natural cycles of night and day (as well as on bird, insect and animal behaviour) and inhibits the observation of stars and planets.

light year the distance light travels through space in one year, equivalent to approximately 9.5 thousand billion kilometres.

magnitude the apparent brightness of an object in the sky as it appears to an observer on Earth; greater values are dimmer stars and vice versa.

maria meaning 'seas'; referring to the large, dark, volcanic plains on the Moon.

Mars fourth planet from the Sun, also known as the 'Red Planet' for its red colour; a terrestrial planet.

Mercury closest planet to the Sun and the smallest in the solar system; a terrestrial planet.

meteor streak of light that occurs when a meteoroid burns up in the Earth's atmosphere; popularly known as a 'shooting star'.

meteor shower the appearance of a group of meteors coming from the same area in the sky, usually the result of Earth passing through the orbit of a comet.

meteorite a rock from space that survives the passage through Earth's atmosphere and falls to the ground.

meteoroid small, rocky and/or icy debris that travels through space.

Milky Way our galaxy; also the name of the milky band we see in the sky that is a part of the galaxy's disc.

nebula a diffuse cloud of gas and dust in space; bright nebulae shine either by reflected starlight or by energy from starlight causing the cloud to glow; dark nebulae are clouds of dust and gas so dense that they block the light from stars behind, so it appears dark.

Neptune eighth planet and furthest from the Sun; a gas giant.

New Moon point in the Moon's orbit when it lies between the Earth and the Sun; as the side of the Moon facing Earth is completely in shadow, the Moon itself is not visible.

Oort Cloud the most distant region of our solar system, believed to be a sphere of comets.

open star cluster a collection of hundreds to thousands of stars travelling together through space in the flat disc of the Milky Way Galaxy.

perigee closest that the Moon comes to the Earth in its orbit; also applies to satellites.

peripheral vision observing technique used by amateur astronomers, involves looking slightly to one side of a faint object so its light falls on the eye's night-sensitive part of the retina; same as averted vision.

Pluto a dwarf planet; until 2006, Pluto was known as the ninth planet.

radiant point in the sky from which meteors appear to originate in a meteor shower.

red giant a dying star in the late stages of stellar evolution; our Sun will become a red giant in about five billion years.

rhodopsin a biological pigment found in the rods of the retina that converts light into electrical signals sent to the brain.

rod cells cells in the eye's retina that are sensitive to dim light, used for night vision.

satellite a natural or artificial (human-made) body orbiting a planet; the Moon is Earth's natural satellite; the International Space Station is an artificial satellite.

Saturn sixth planet from the Sun, one of the naked-eye planets; the second largest planet in the solar system, best known for its distinctive rings.

sonic boom explosive sound caused by the shockwave generated by an object travelling faster than the speed of sound.

space junk collection of artificial (human-made) objects floating in space, also known as space debris and space waste.

star a self-luminous sphere of hot gas, predominantly hydrogen, held together by gravity; the Sun is a star.

subgiant a star brighter than our Sun but dimmer than a giant star.

Sun the star at the centre of our solar system, around which the Earth orbits.

sunspot darker, cooler spot on the surface of the Sun.

supergiant the largest kind of star in the universe; supergiants can be hundreds of times larger than our Sun and are prone to exploding as supernovas.

supermoon a Full Moon or a New Moon at or near the point of perigee.

supernova a huge explosion that occurs at the end of a heavy star's life.

terrestrial planet the inner solar system's rocky planets; there are four of them: Mercury, Venus, Earth and Mars; they orbit closer to the Sun than the gas giant planets.

total lunar eclipse when the Earth's shadow falls on the Moon because the Earth is between the Sun and the Moon.

total solar eclipse when the Moon blocks the light from the Sun because the Moon is between the Sun and the Earth.

Uranus seventh planet from the Sun; gas giant.

variable star a star whose brightness changes over time.

Venus second planet from the Sun; a terrestrial planet often called the 'sister' to the Earth because it is very similar to Earth in size and composition.

waning referring to the phases of the Moon (between Full Moon and New Moon), when the illuminated section appears to reduce in size as seen from Earth.

waxing referring to the phases of the Moon (between New Moon and Full Moon), when the illuminated section appears to grow in size as seen from Earth.

zenith the point overhead.

zodiac the region in the sky (the ecliptic) along which the Sun, Moon and planets move; it also refers to the 12 constellations through which the Sun, Moon and planets pass on their journeys around the Sun.

zodiacal light a faint elongated cone of light sometimes seen in the night sky, extending from the horizon along the ecliptic.

Appendix: Stars, constellations and deep-sky objects

This alphabetical list is a guide to the months in which these celestial objects are described in detail.

47 Tucanae (November)
Acamar (December)
Achernar (December)
Albireo (September)
Aldebaran (January)
Algieba (April)
Algol (January)
Almach (December)
Alnair (October)
Alpha Centauri (June)
Alpha Persei Cluster (January)
Alphard (March)
Alphecca (June)
Altair (September)
Andromeda (November)
Andromeda Galaxy (November)
Antares (July)
Aquarius (September)
Aquila (September)
Ara the Altar (July; August)
Arcturus (June)
Argo Navis (February)
Aries (December)
Auriga (February)
Beehive Cluster (March)
Belt of Orion (February)
Berenice's Hair (May)
Beta Centauri (June)
Betelgeuse (February)
Big Dipper (April)
Boötes (May)
Canes Venatici (May)
Canopus (February)
Capella (February)
Capricornus (September; October)
Cassiopeia (November)
Castor (March)
Centaurus (May)
Cetus (September; October; December)
Circlet of Pisces (September; October)
Coalsack Nebula (May)
Coma Berenices (May)
Cor Caroli (May)
Corona Australis (August)
Corona Borealis (June)
Corvus the Crow (May)
Cygnus (September)

Delphinus (September)
Deneb (September)
Deneb Kaitos (November)
Denebola (April)
Diamond Cross (March; April)
Dragon's Head (Draco) (August)
Enif (October)
Eridanus the River (November; December)
Eta Carinae & Nebula (April)
False Comet (July)
False Cross (March)
Fomalhaut (October)
Gemini (March)
Great Square of Pegasus (October)
Great Sagittarius Star Cloud (August)
Grus the Crane (October)
Hamal (December)
Hyades (January)
Hydra (March)
Hydrus (January)
IC 2602 (Southern Pleiades) (April)
Job's Coffin (September)
Keystone of Hercules (July)
Lagoon Nebula (August)
Large Magellanic Cloud (January, February)
Leo (April)
Libra (June)
Lupus (June)
M4 (July)
M6 (July)
M7 (July)
M8 (August)
M13 (July)
M20 (August)
M22 (August)
M24 (August)
M25 (August)
M44 (Beehive; Praesepe) (March)
Menkar (December)
Mira (December)
Mirach (November)
Mirfak (January)
Musca the Fly (May)

NGC 2516 (Southern Beehive) (March)
NGC 3114 (April)
NGC 3532 (April)
Northern Triangle (December)
Omega Centauri (May)
Ophiuchus (August)
Orion's Belt & Sword (February)
Pavo the Peacock (October)
Pin Cushion Cluster (NGC 3532) (April)
Pisces (September)
Piscis Austrinis (September)
Pleiades (January)
Pollux (March)
Praesepe (Beehive; M44) (March)
Procyon (March)
Rasalhague (August)
Regulus (April)
Reticulum (January)
Rigel (February)
Sagittarius (August)
Salt Shaker (August)
Scorpius (July)
Sickle of Leo (April)
Sirius (February)
Small Magellanic Cloud (January; November)
Small Sagittarius Star Cloud (M24) (August)
Southern Beehive (NGC 2516) (March)
Southern Cross (February)
Southern Crown (August)
Southern Pleiades (IC 2602) (April)
Spica (April)
Taurus (January)
Teapot (August)
Trifid Nebulae (M20) (August)
Ursa Major (April)
Vega (August)
Virgo (April)
Water Jar of Aquarius (September; October)
Zeta Reticuli (January)
Zubenelgenubi (June)
Zubeneschamali (June)

Index